Dametria & Moreese Strong

Always & Forever

Wedding Procession

The Lord's Prayer by: Taleisha Watson

Announcement of the Bride & Groom

Song: Roberta Flack

Song by Christina Jackson

Dance by Maleness Mathis

(Meal)

Soft Jazz

Couple First Dance

Minister Augusta Mathis

(Coordinator)

Parents of the **B**ride

Min. Augusta & Melvin Mathis

Grandparents of the Bride

Arthur Lee Whitney

Willie Mae Whitney

Andrew Earl White

Raymond Mathis

Viver Ree Mathis

Parents of Groom

Charlotte Johnson

John Johnson

Moreese Strong Sr

We're like a flower to a tree

Like words to a melody

No words that could make us blow

We are inseparable

It's so wonderful

To know you'll always be there.

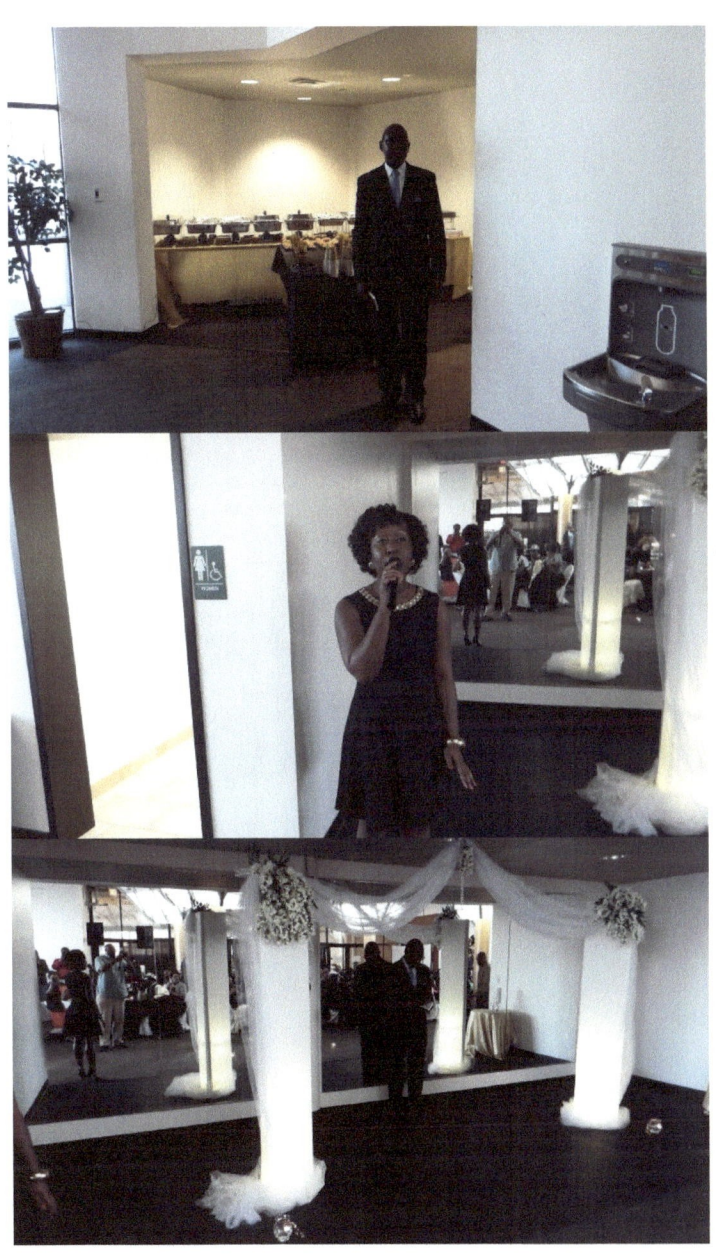

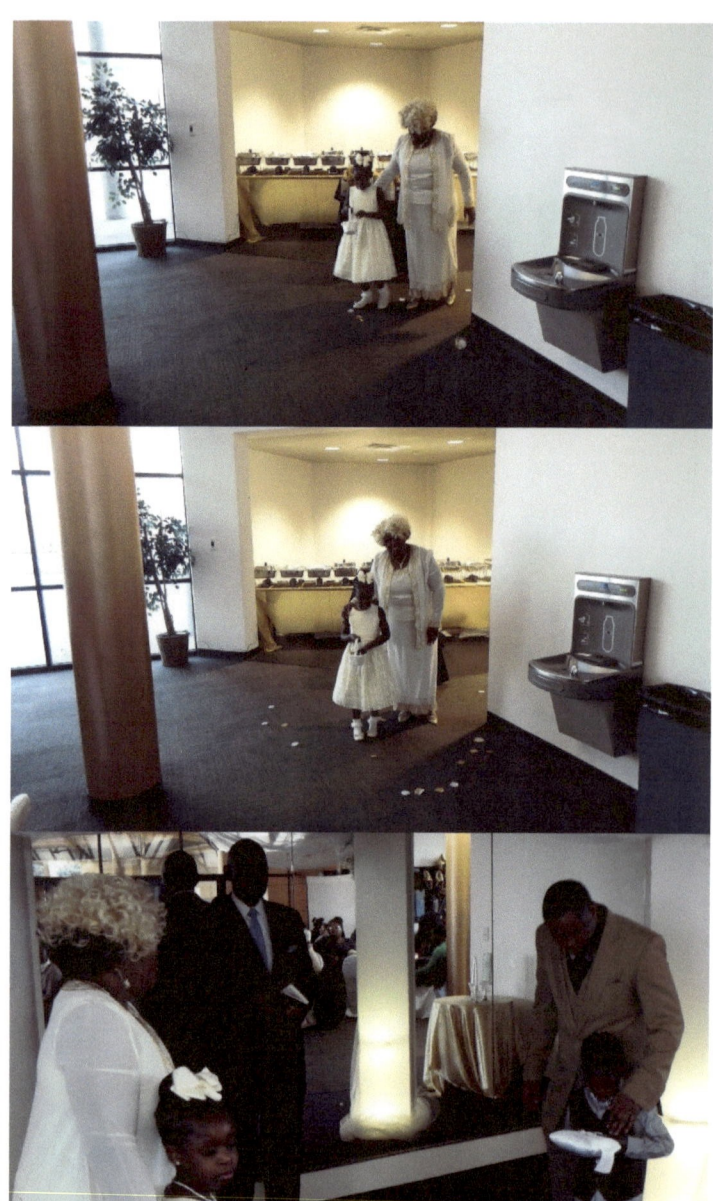

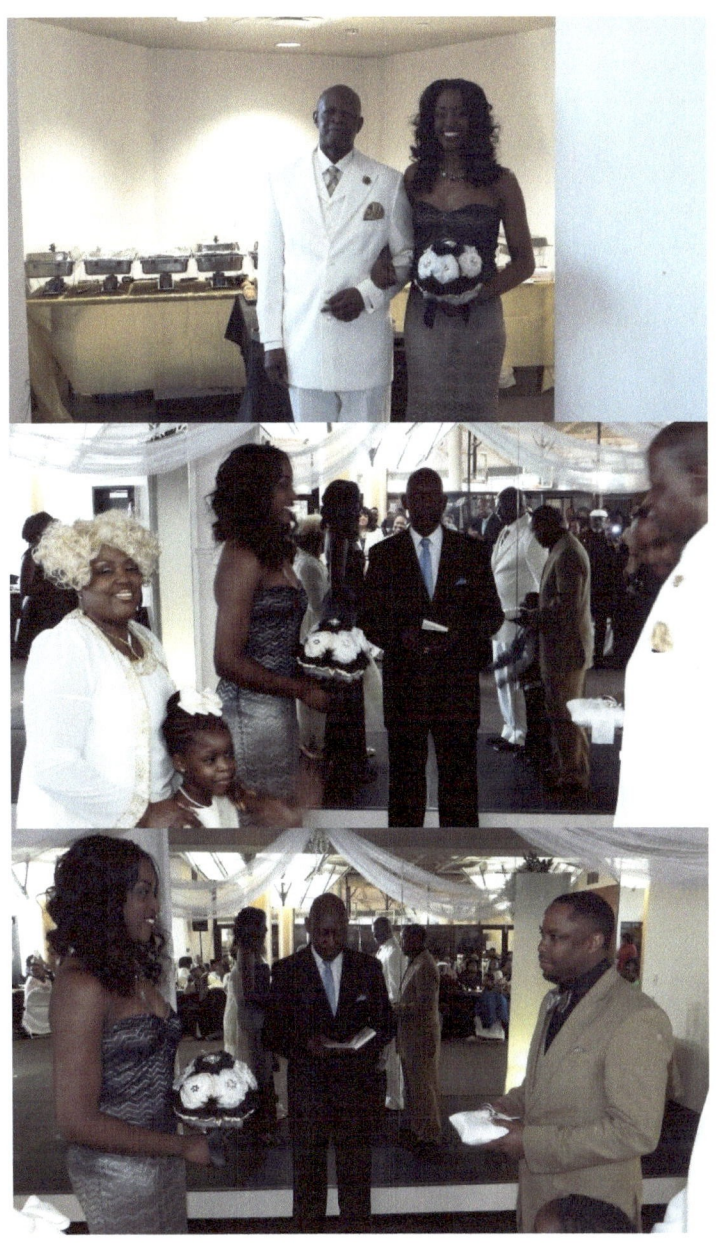

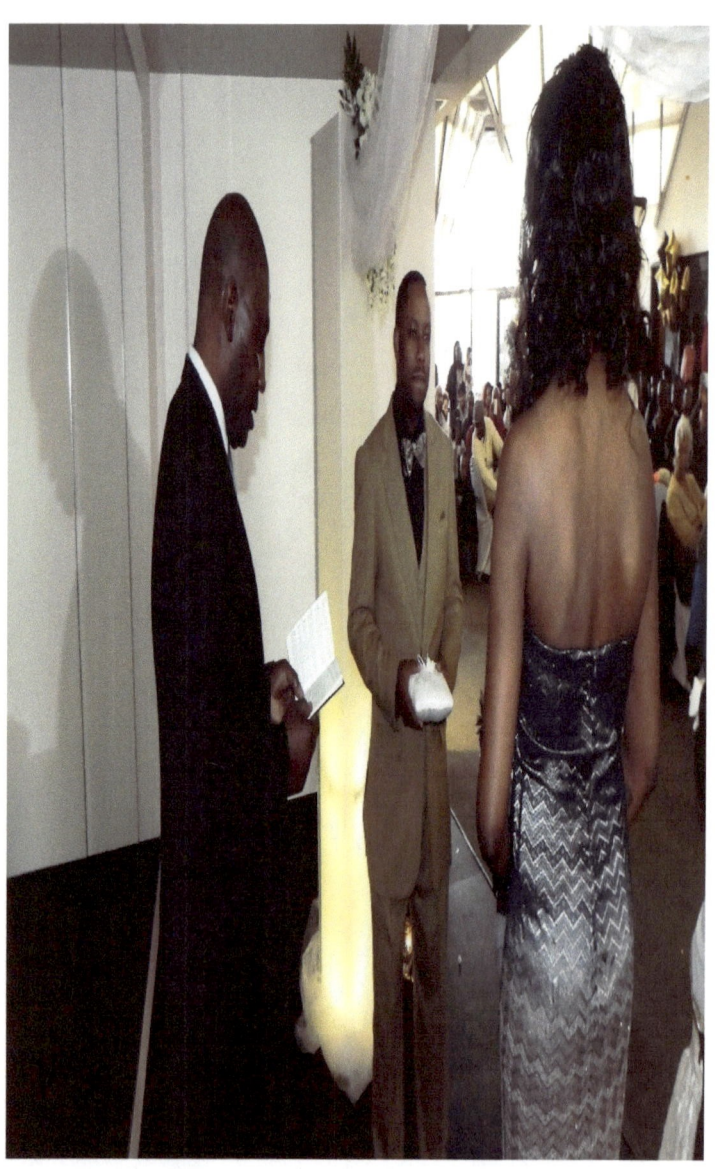

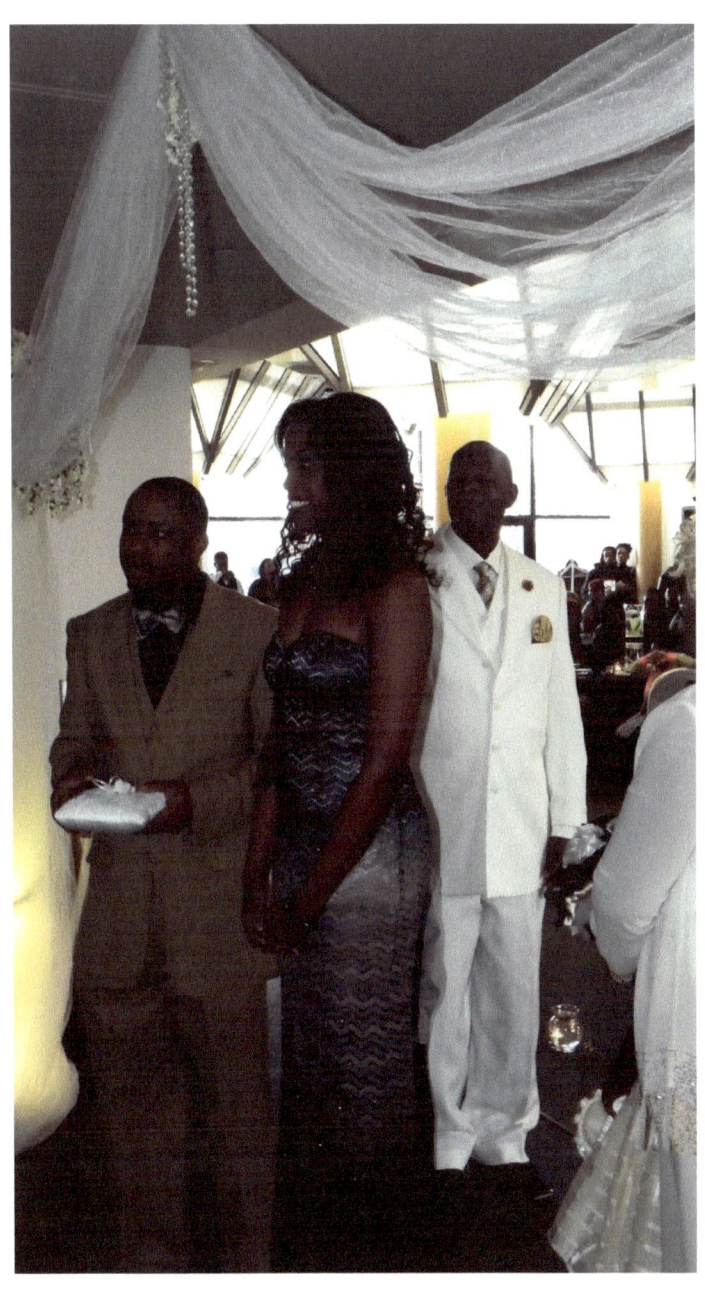

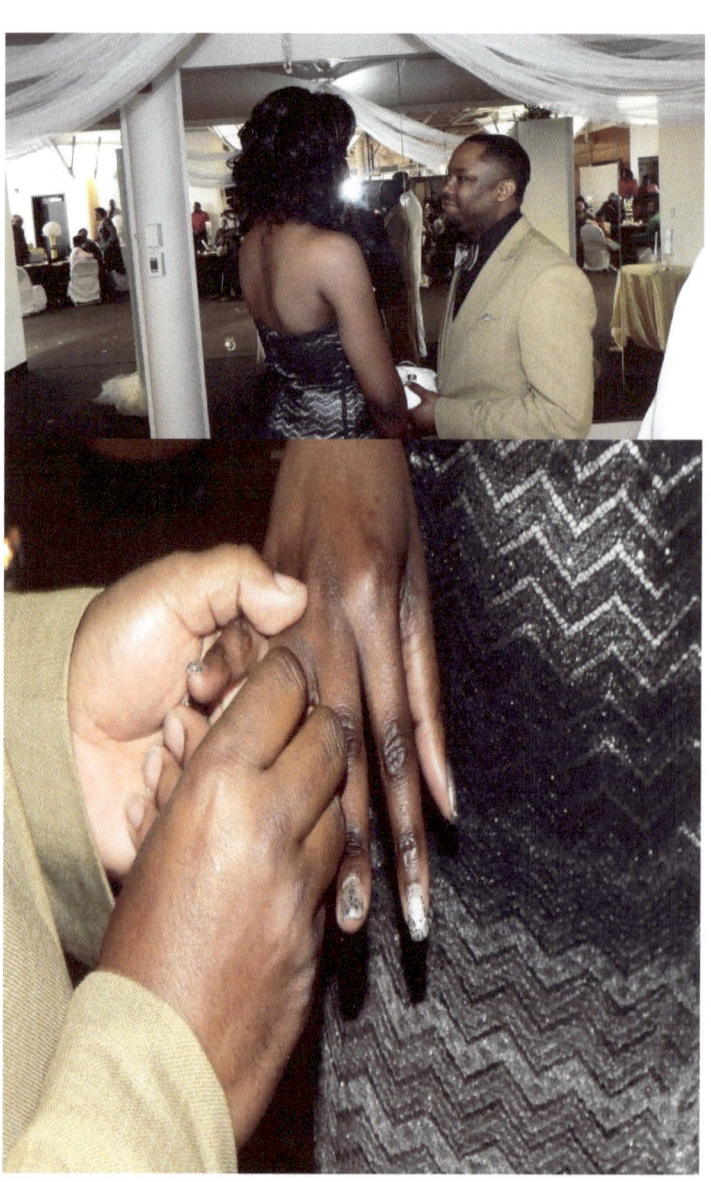

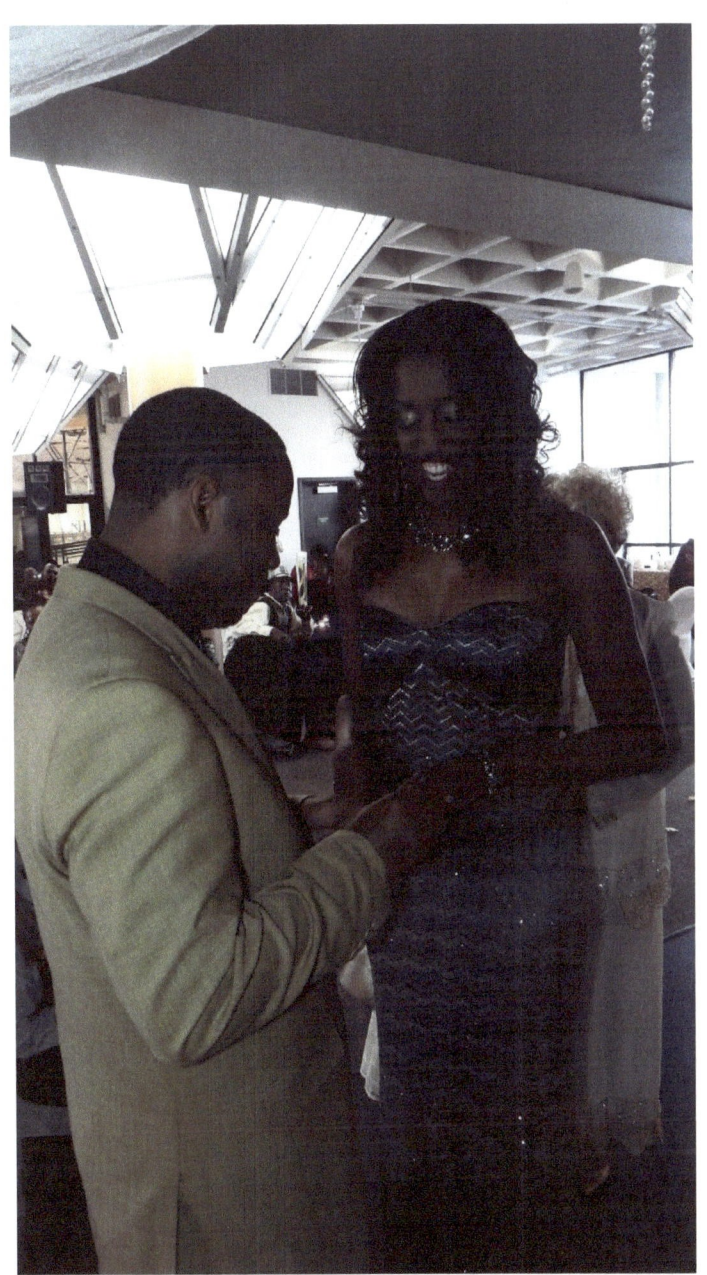

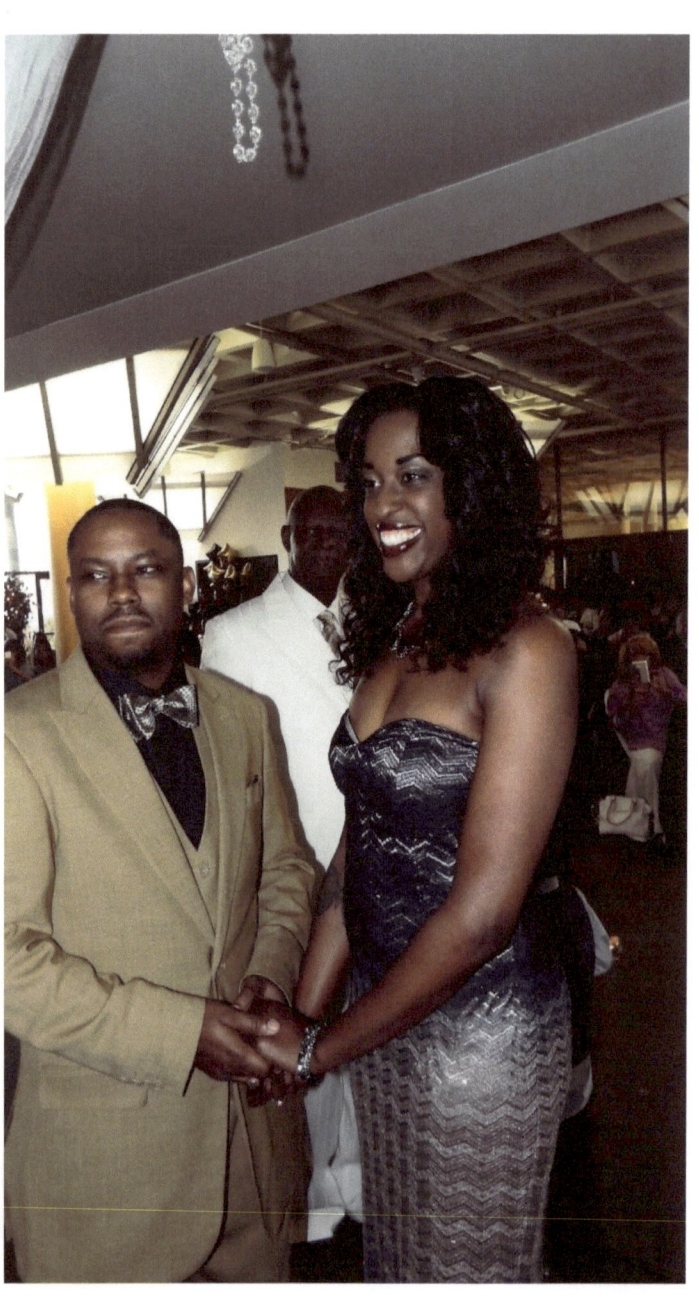

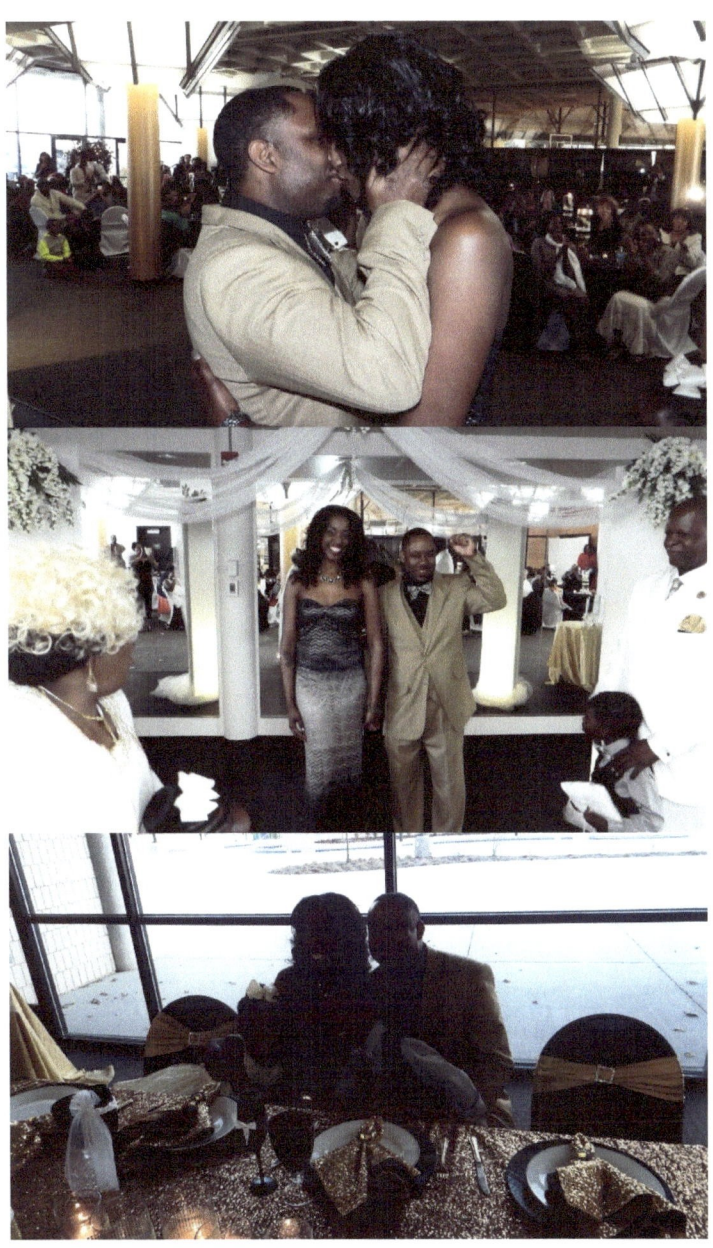

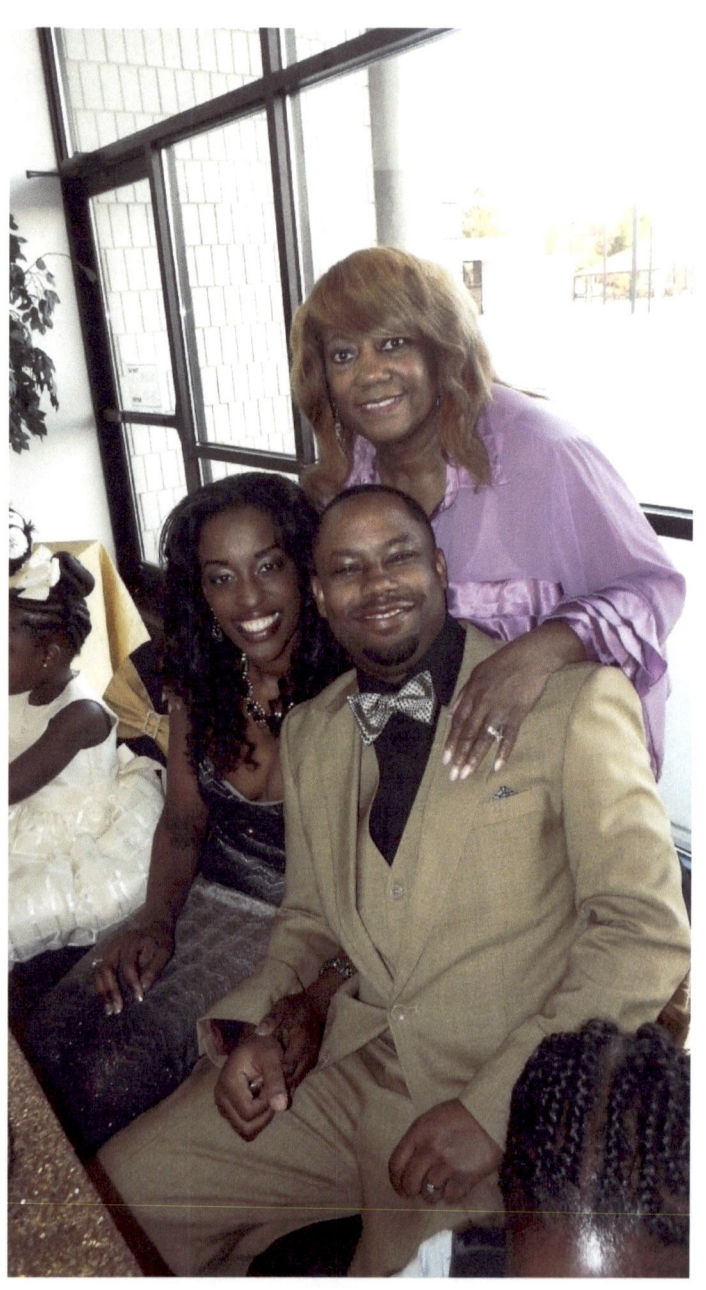

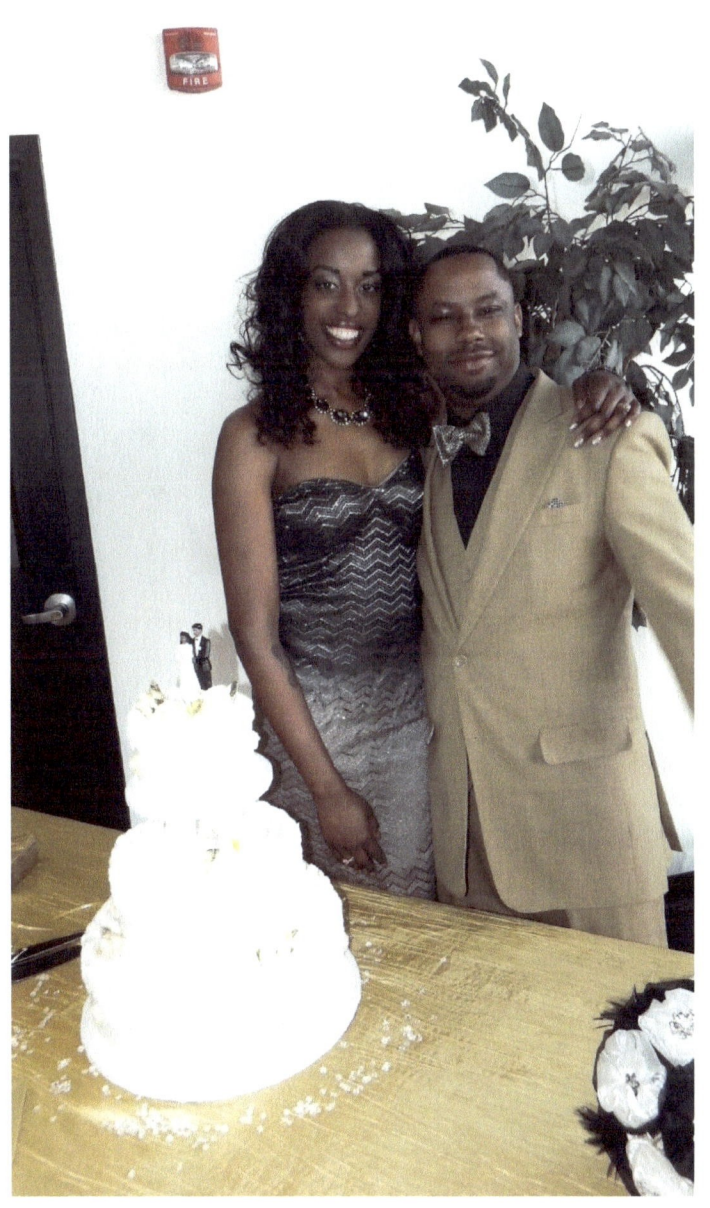

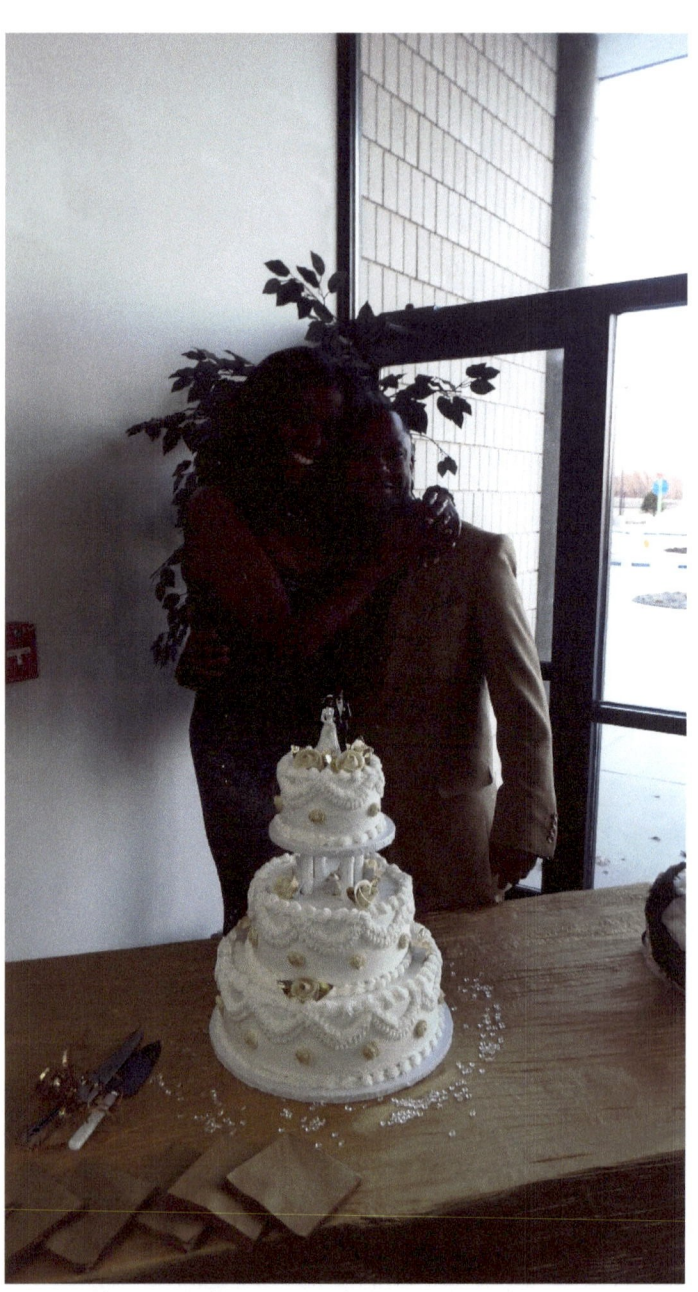

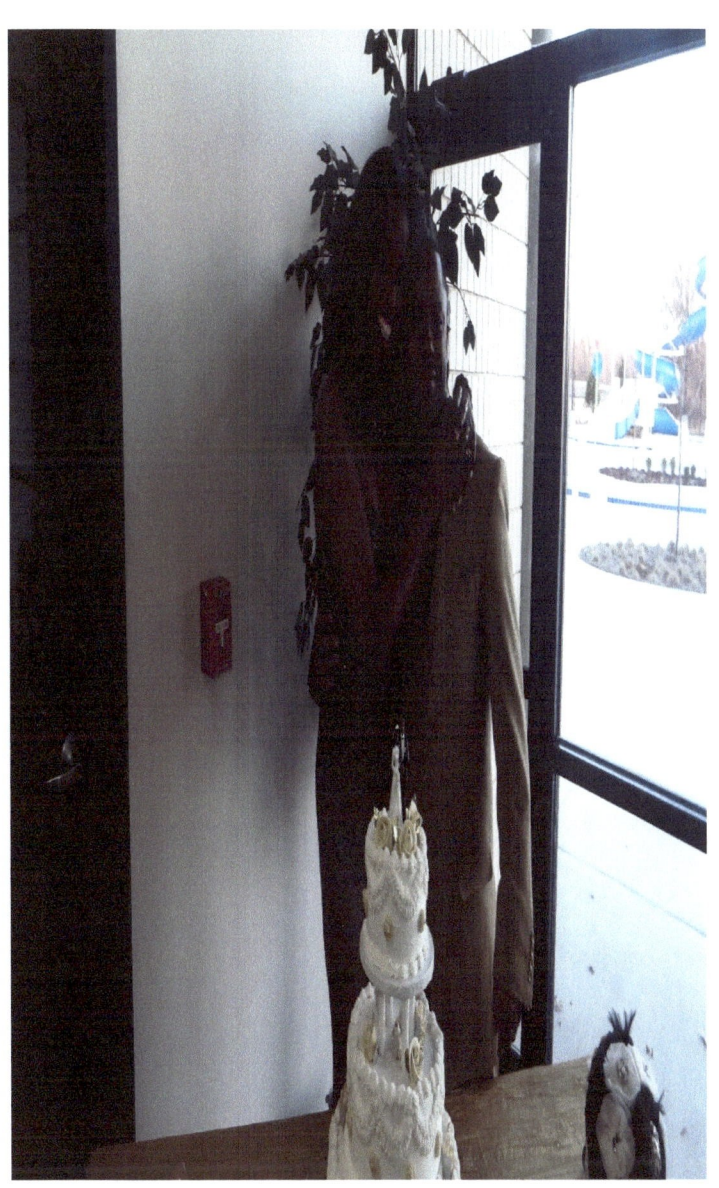

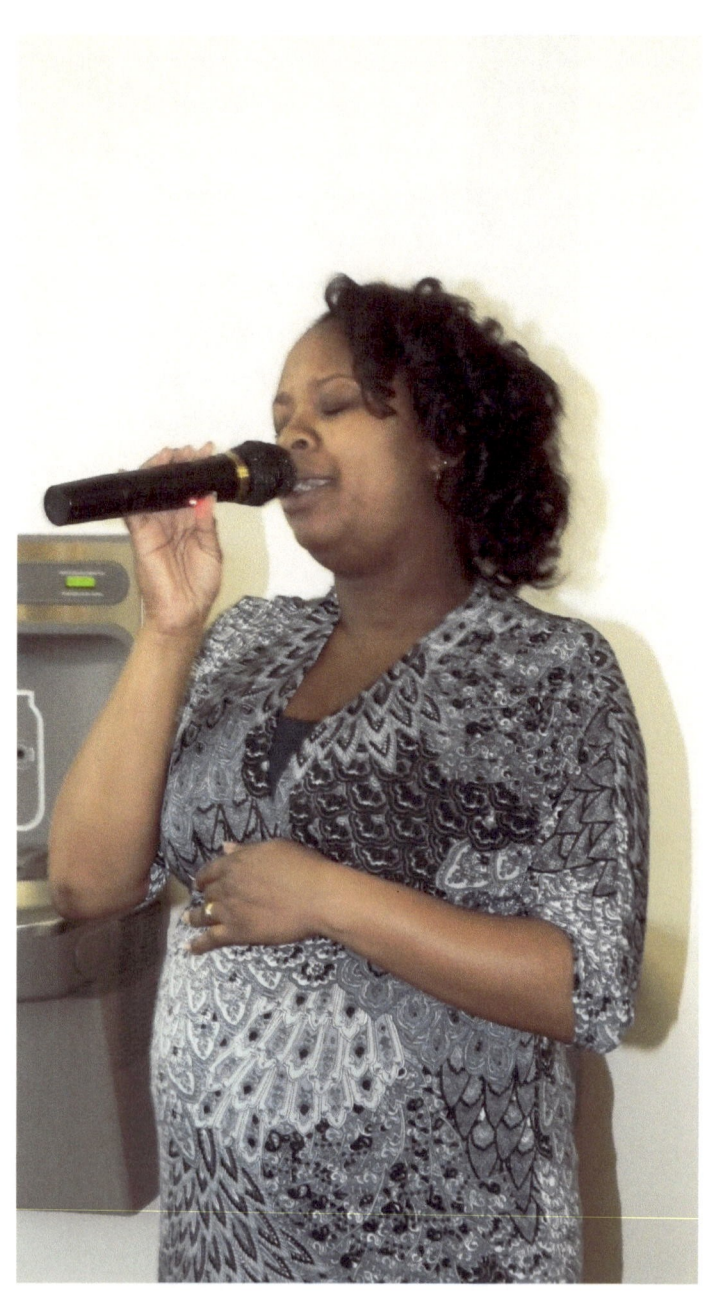

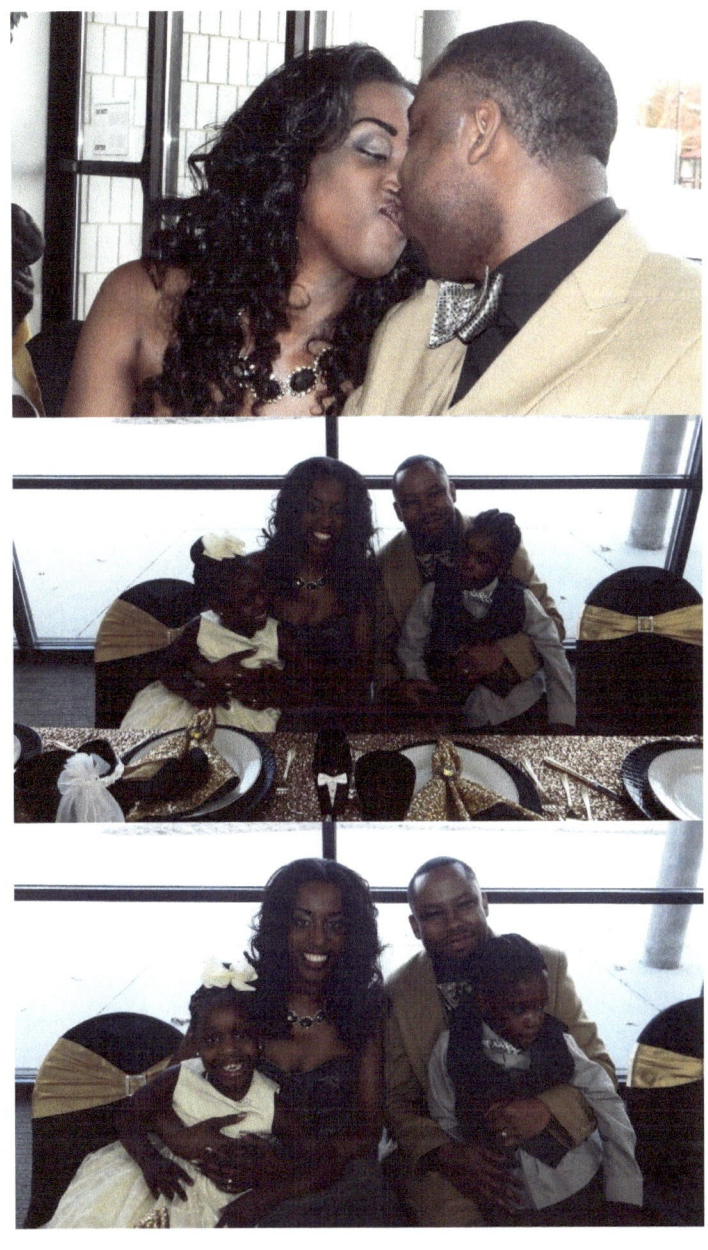

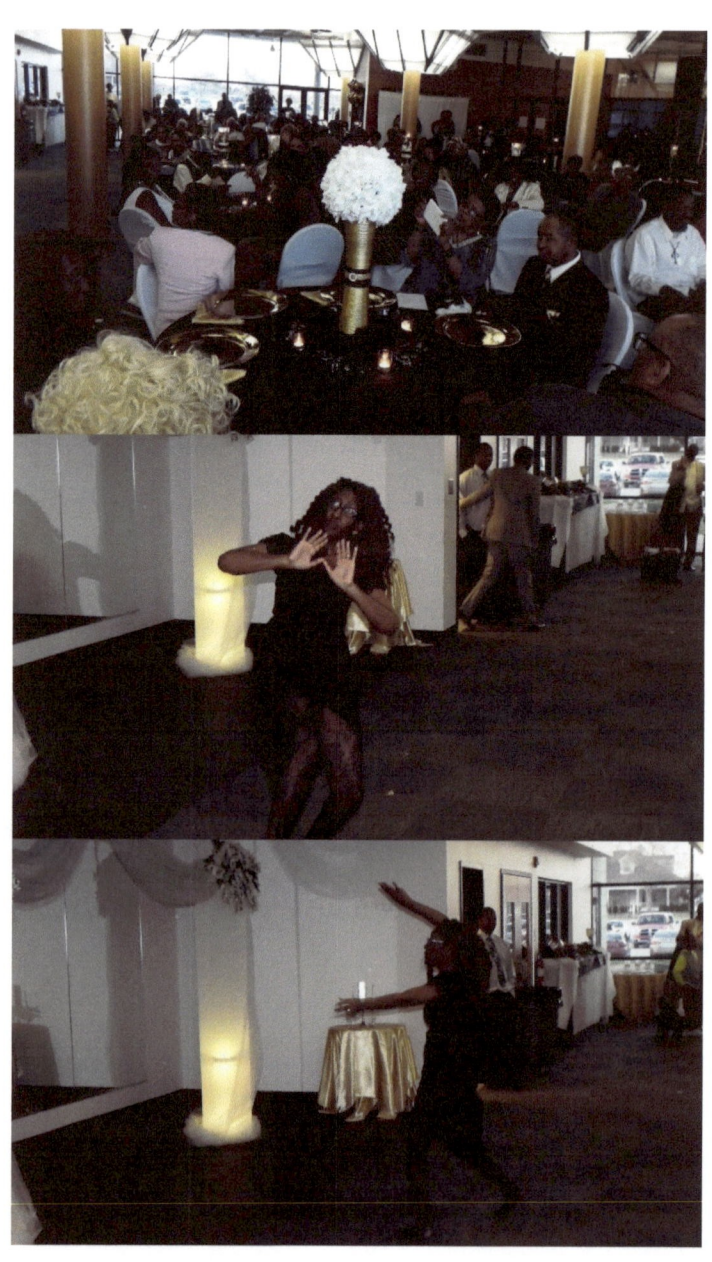

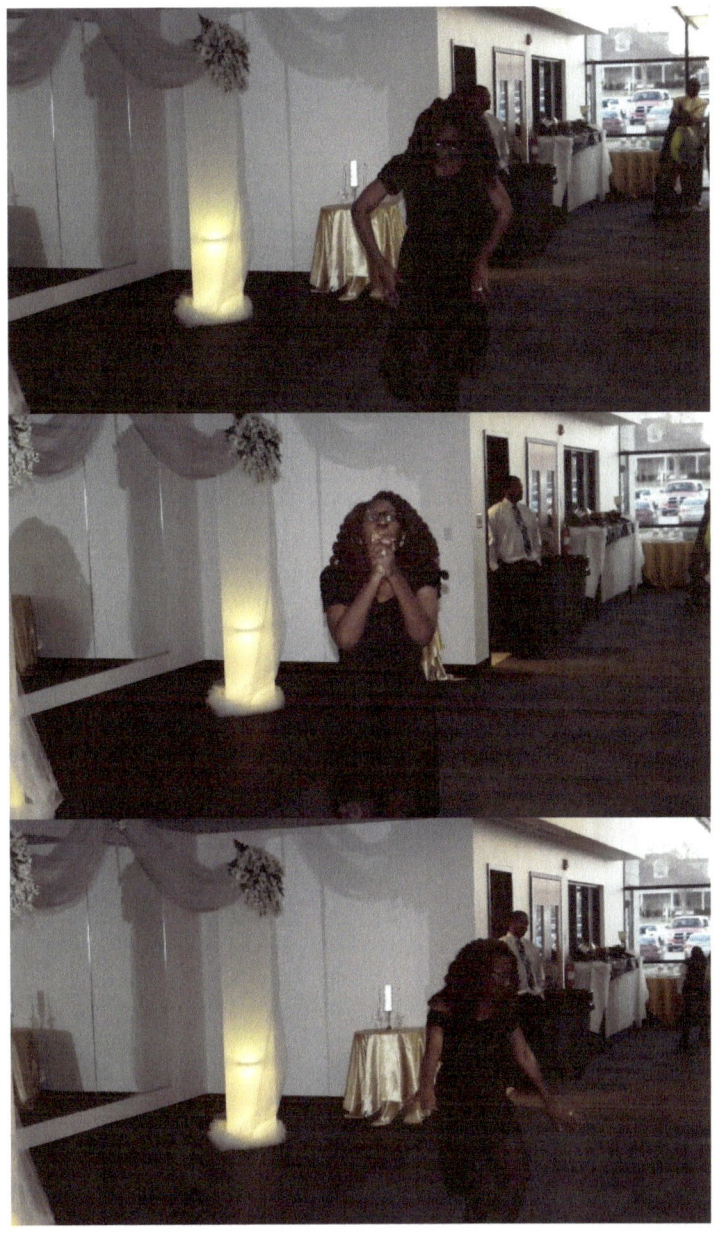

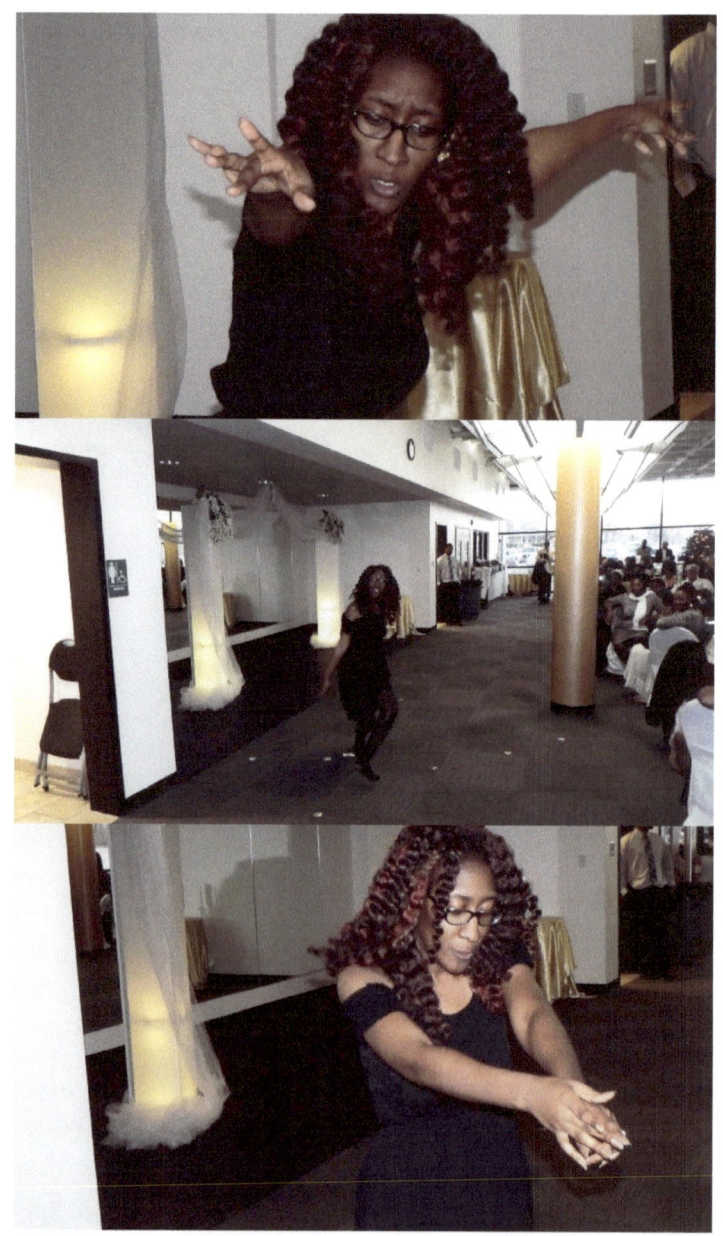

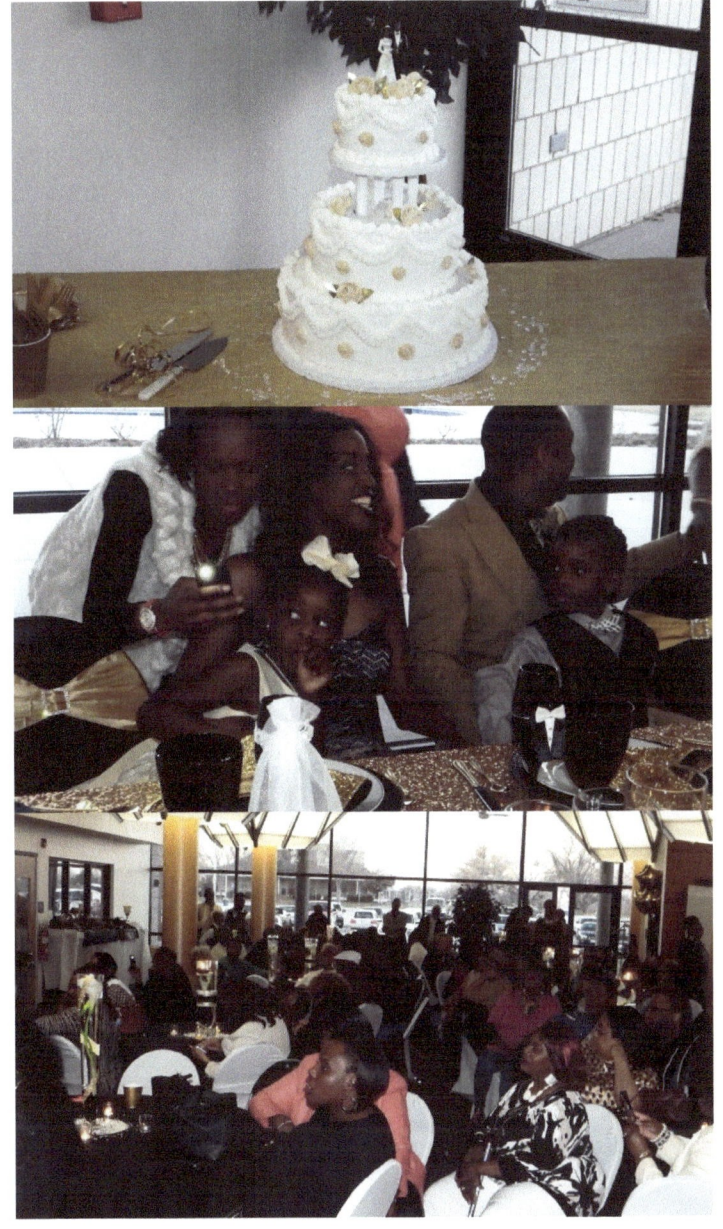

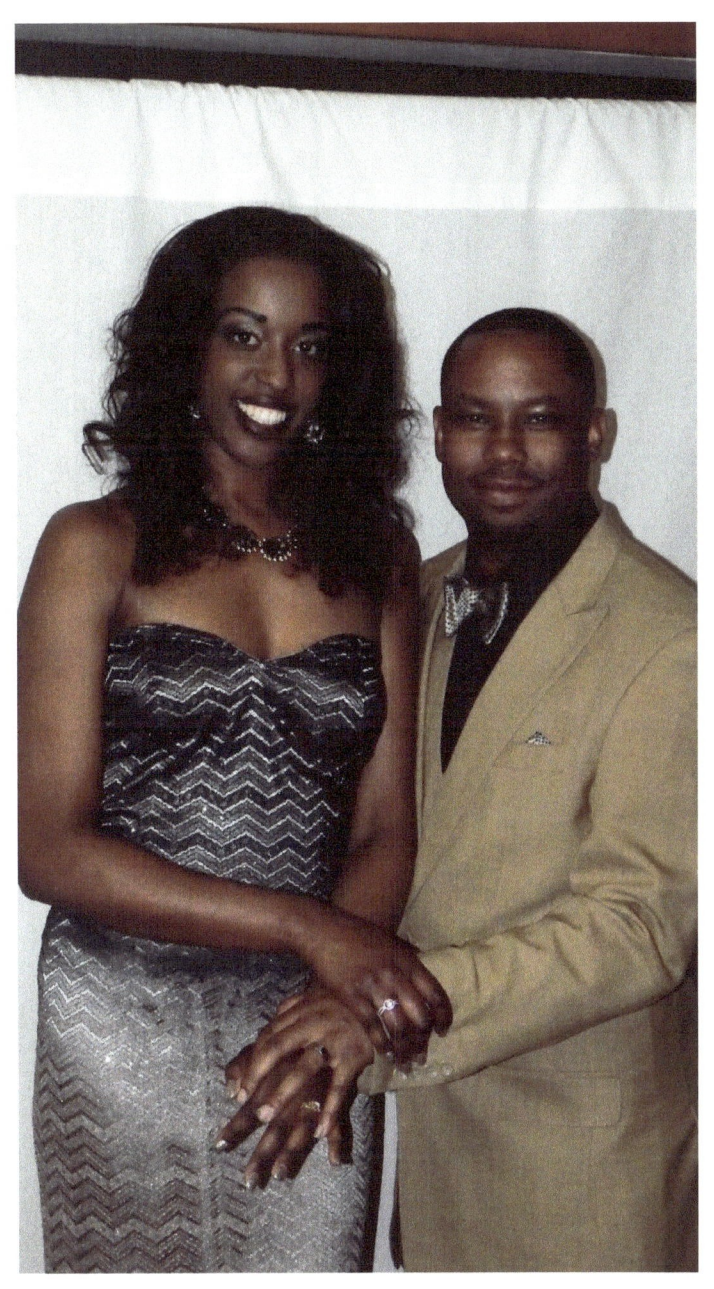

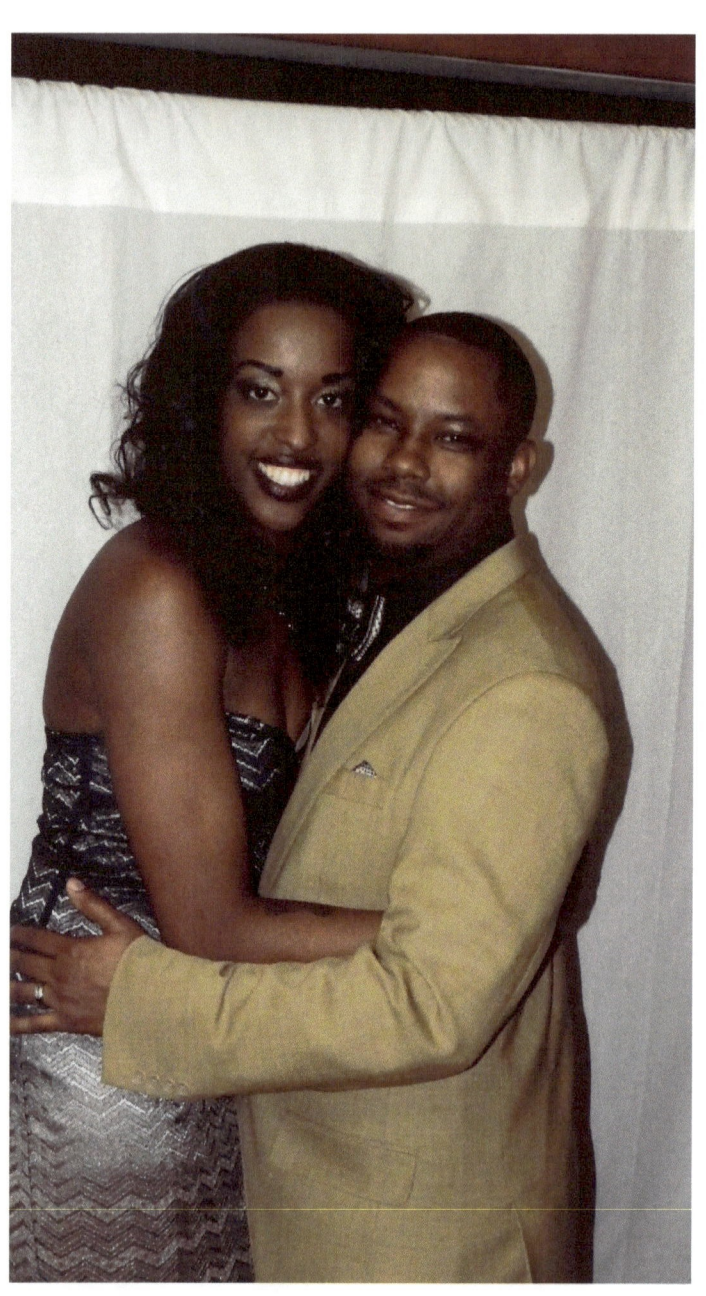

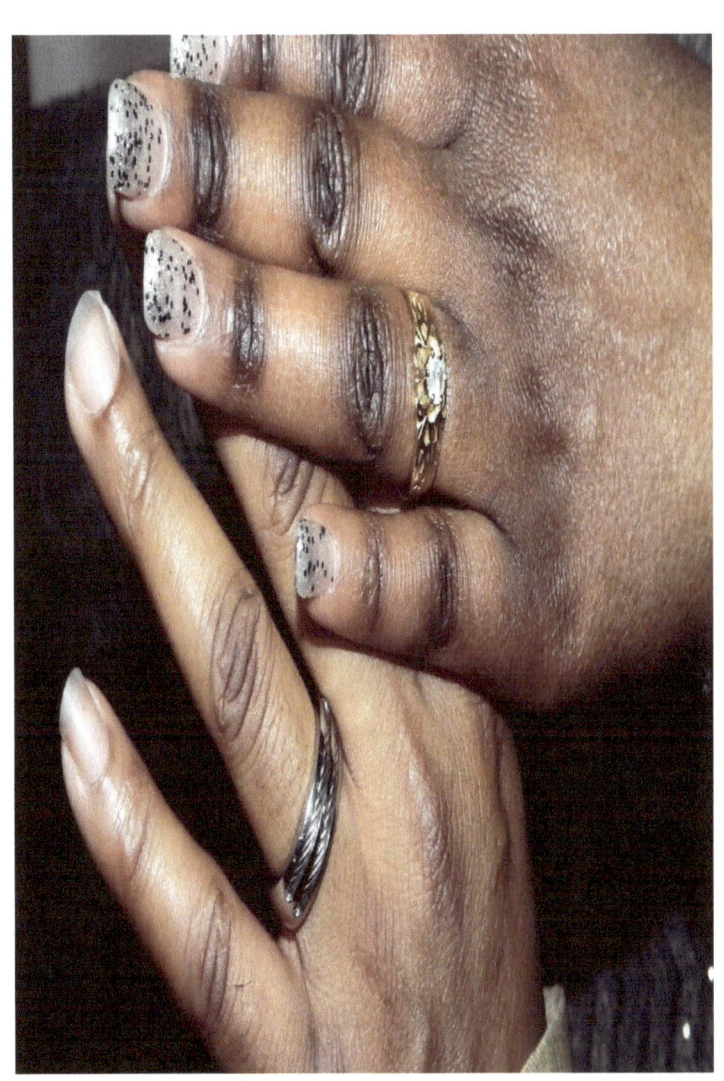

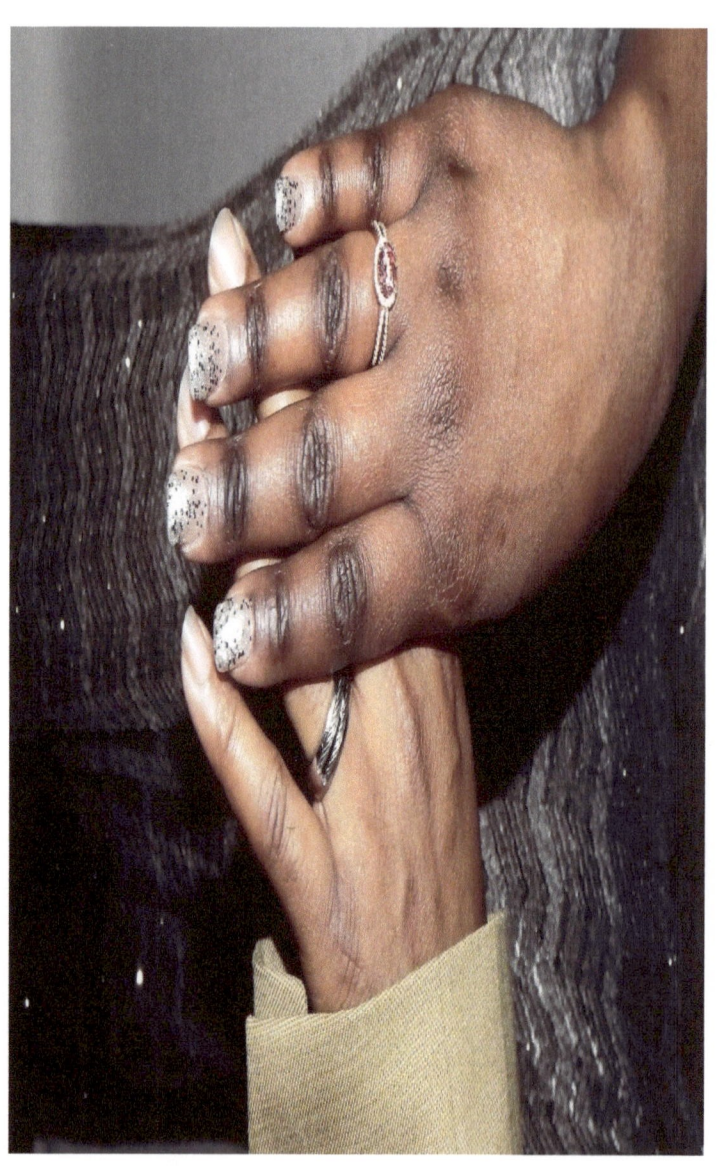

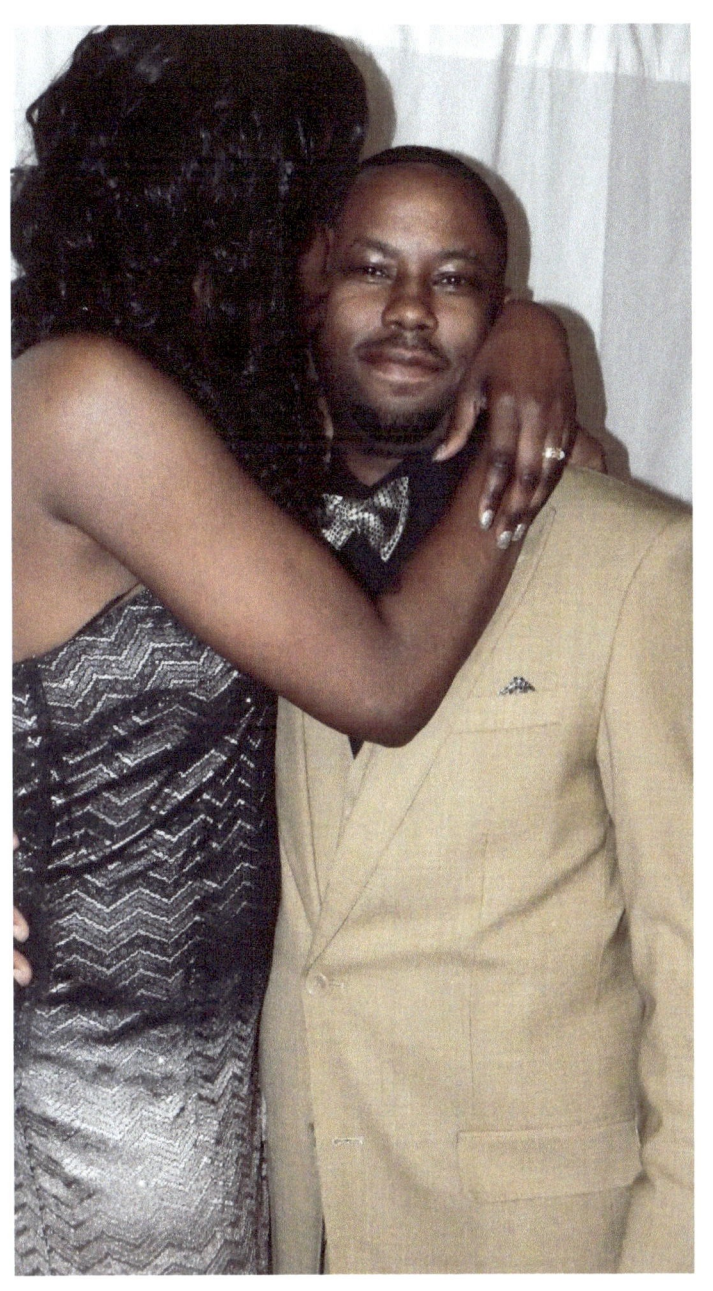

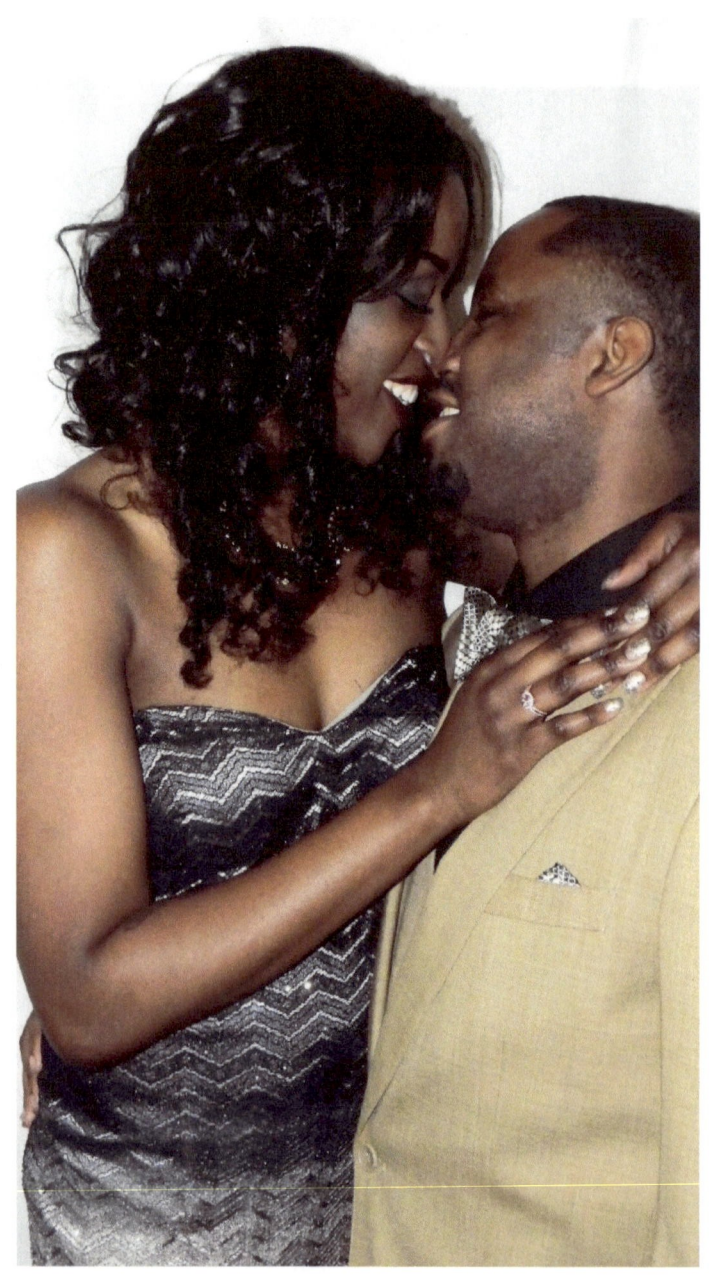

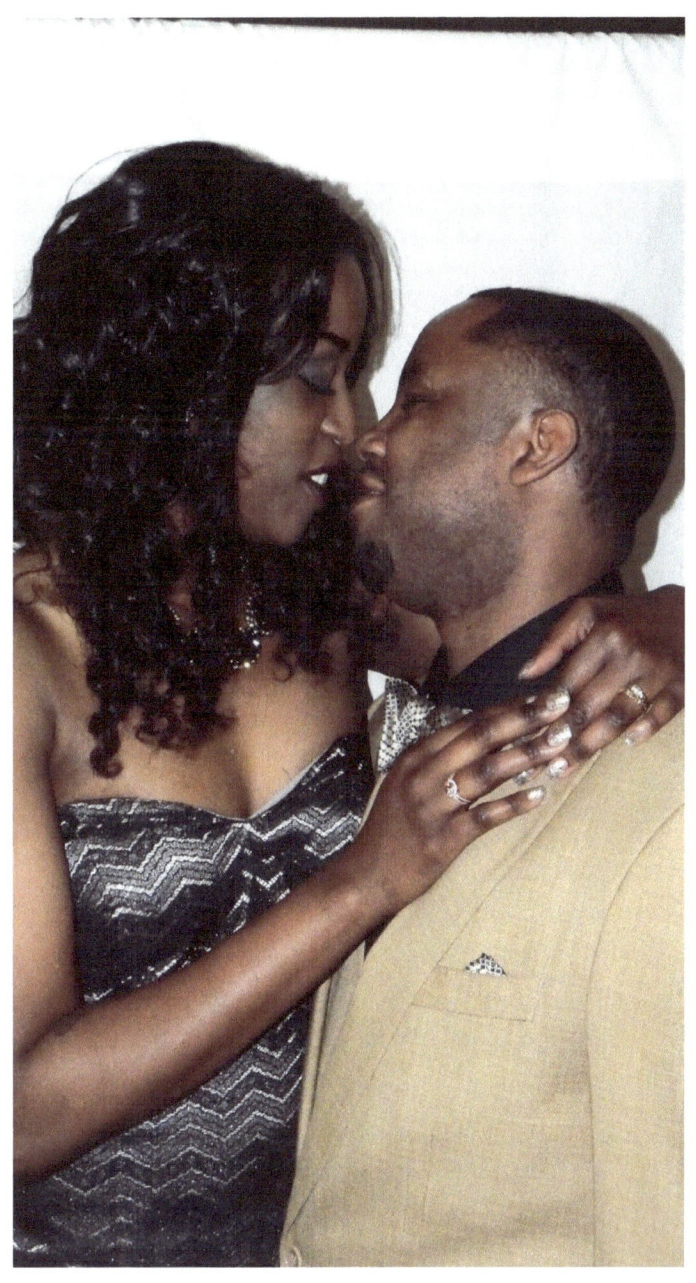

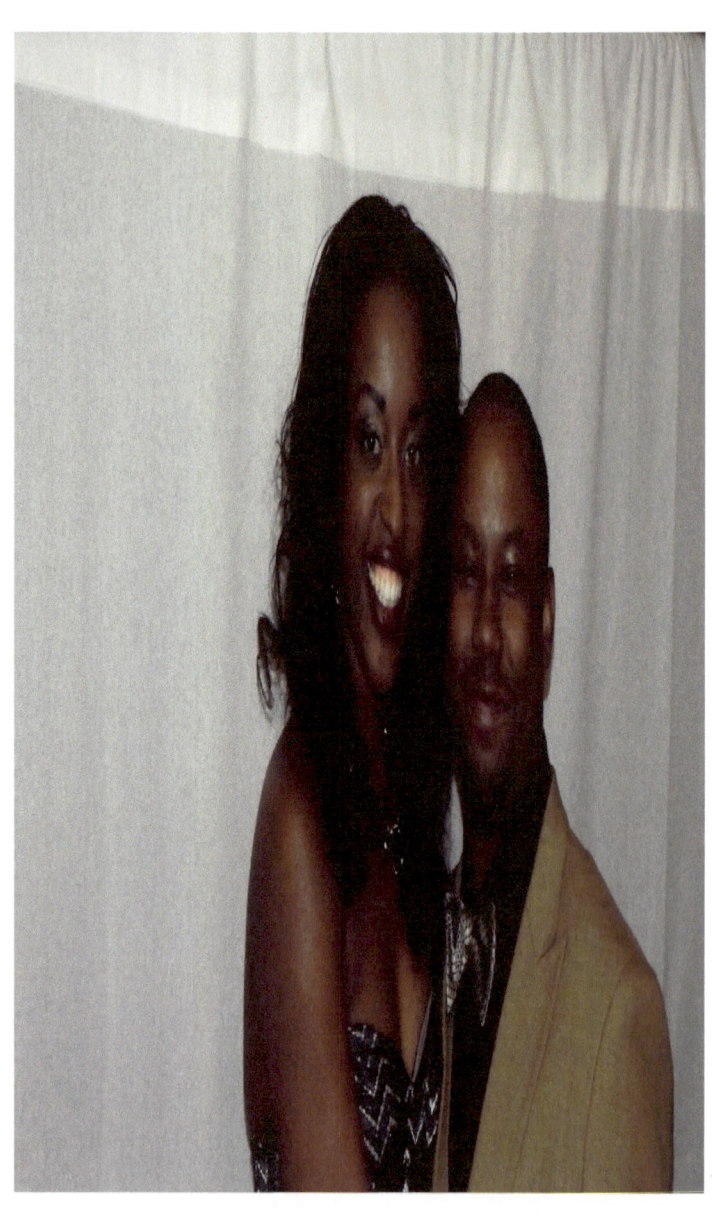

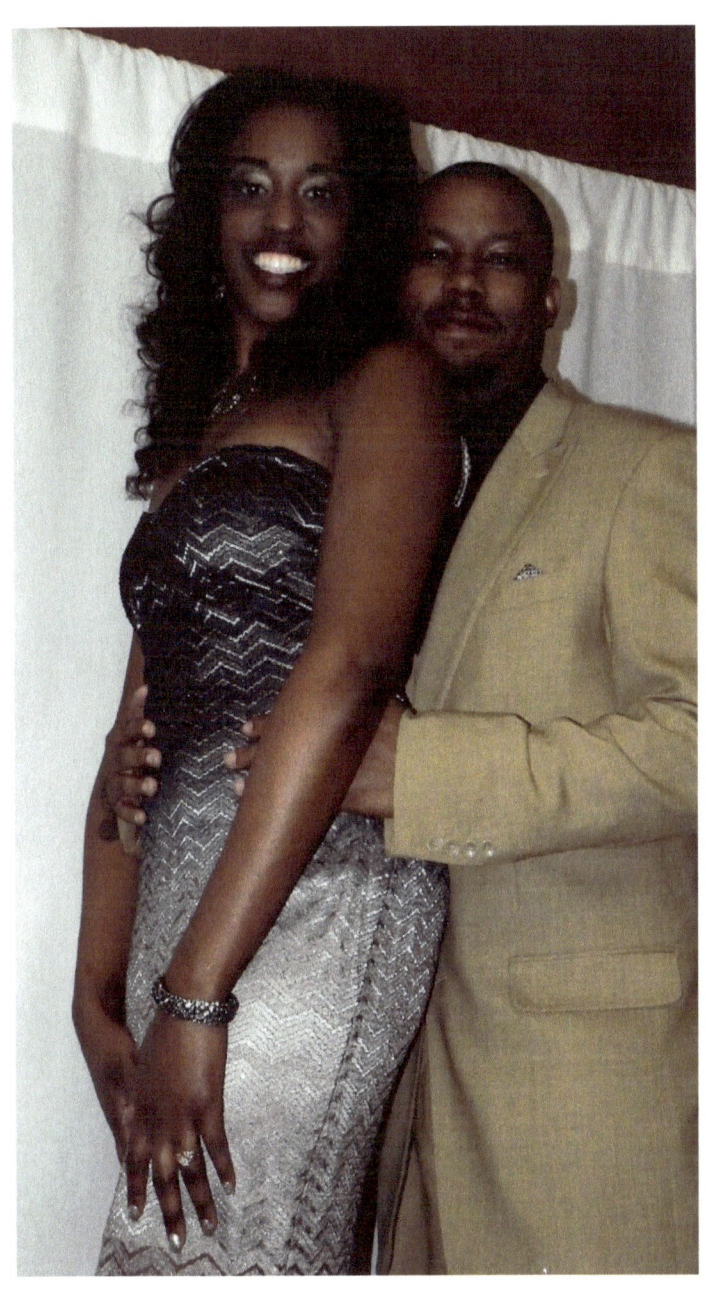

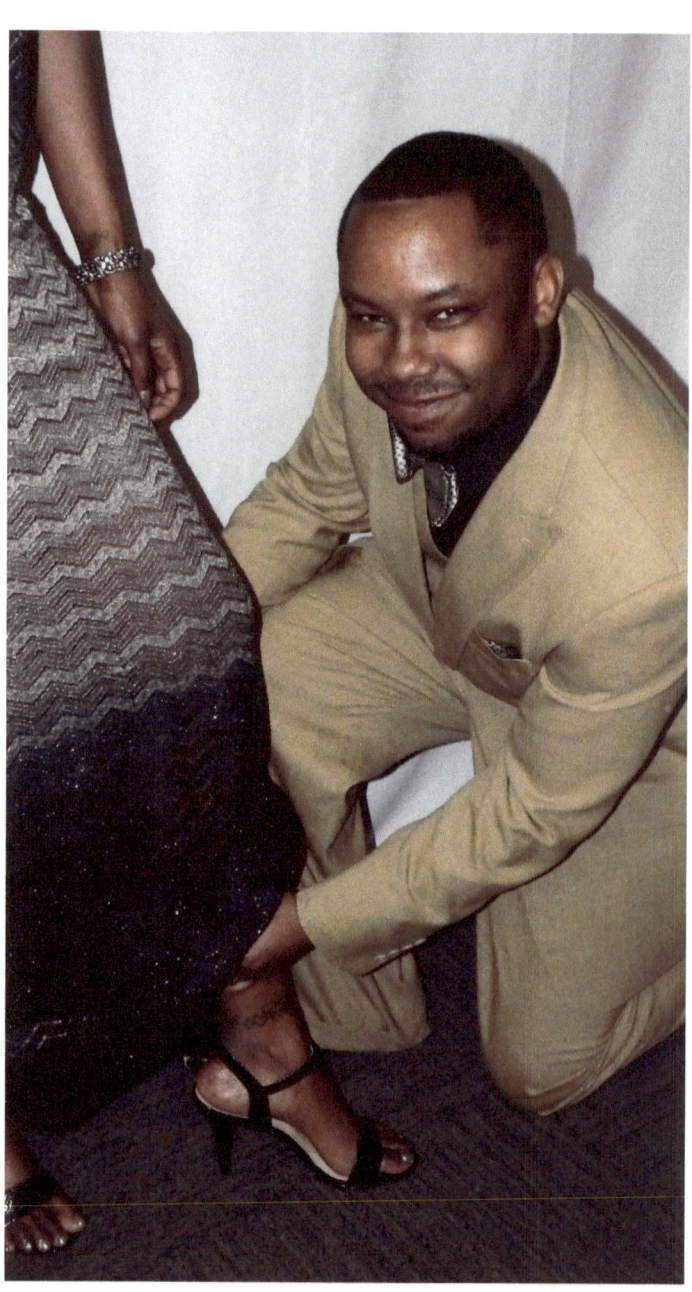

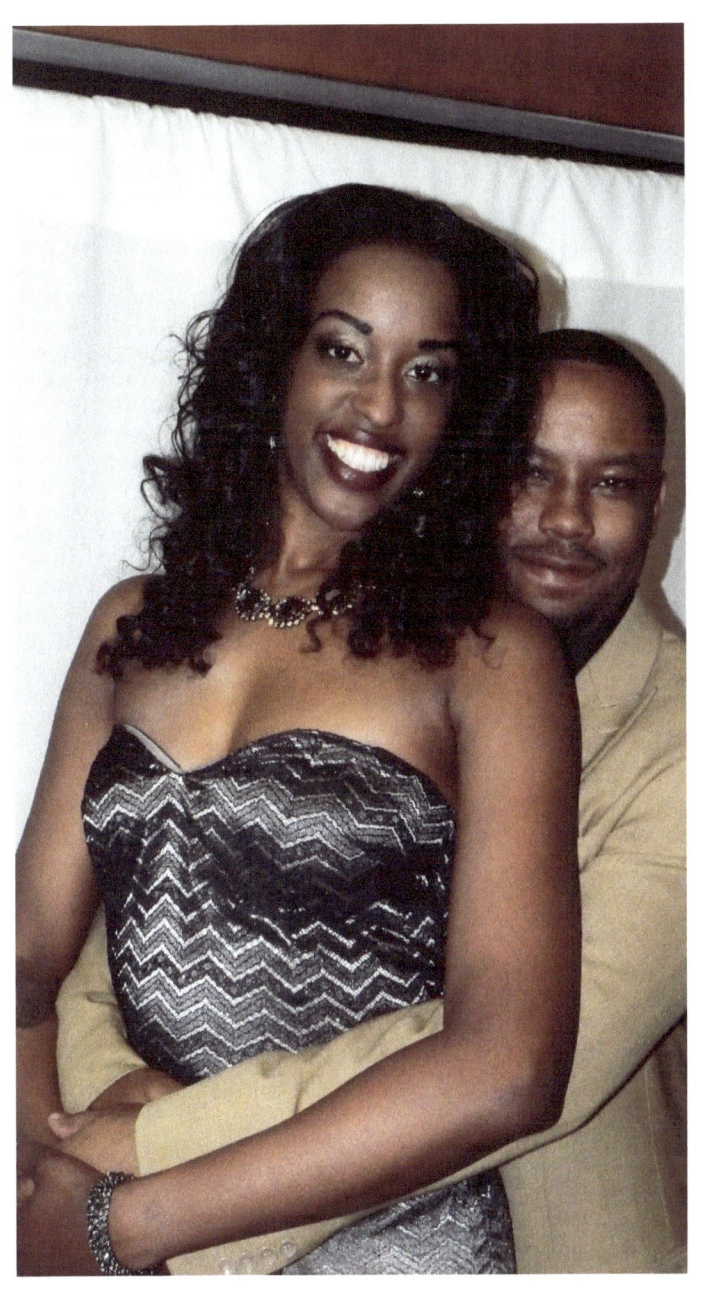

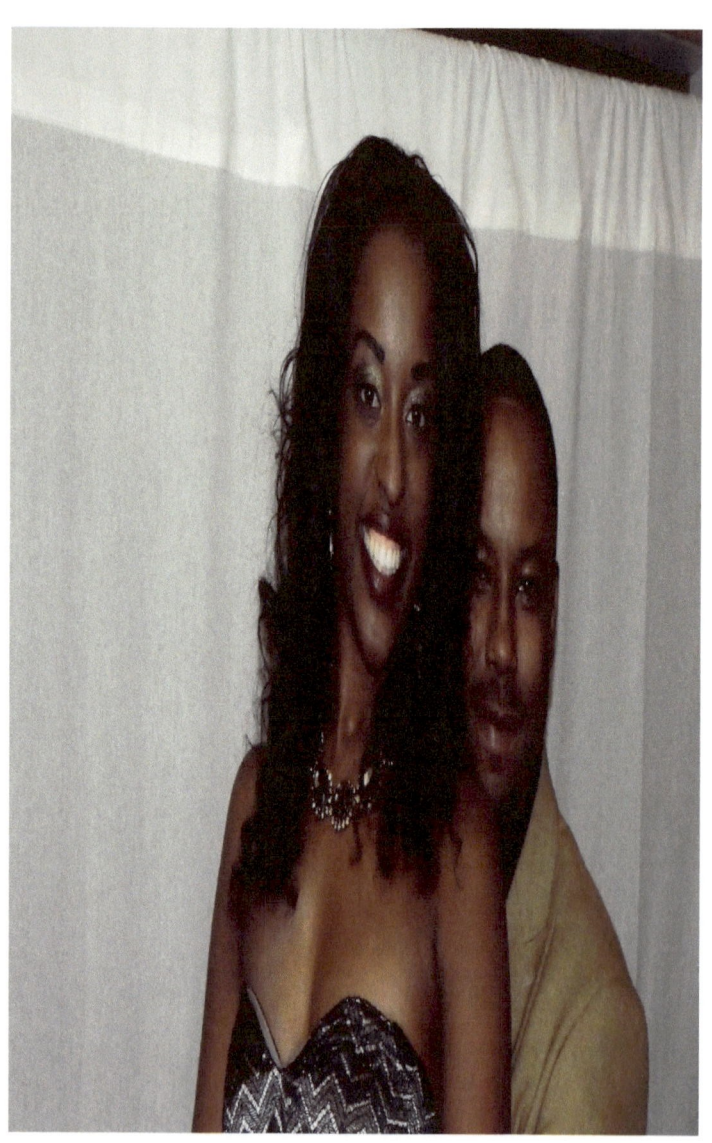

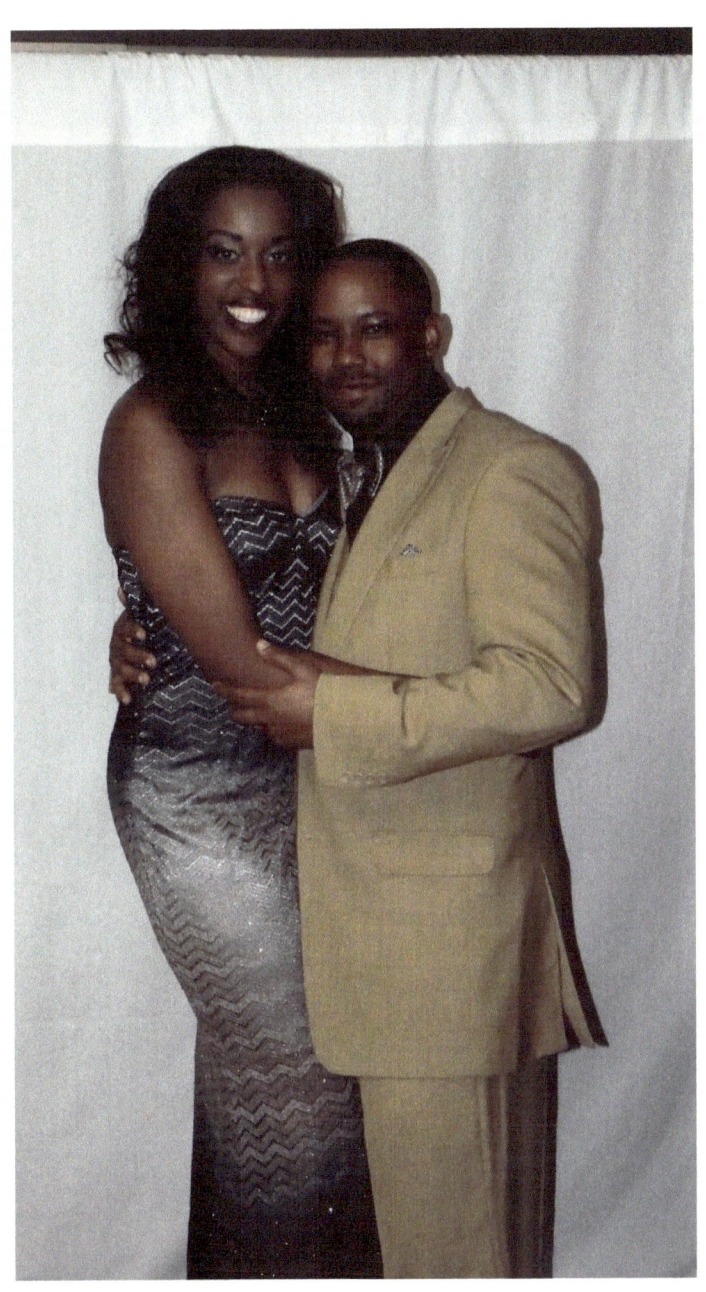

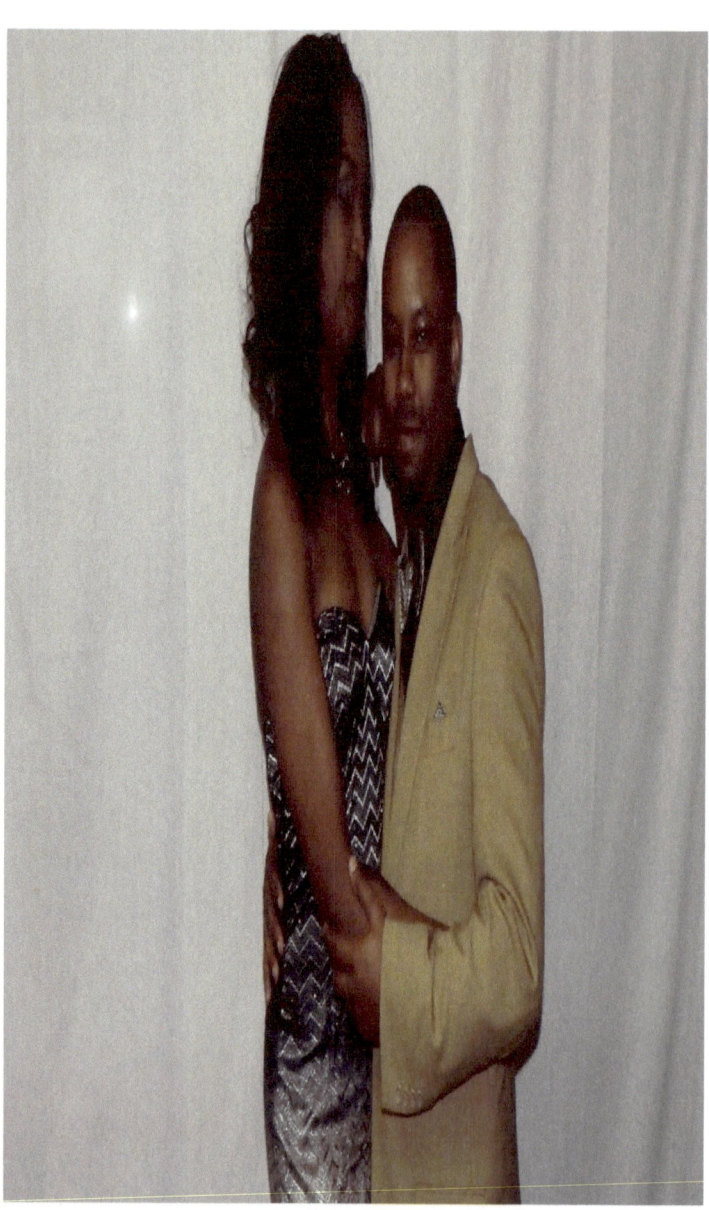

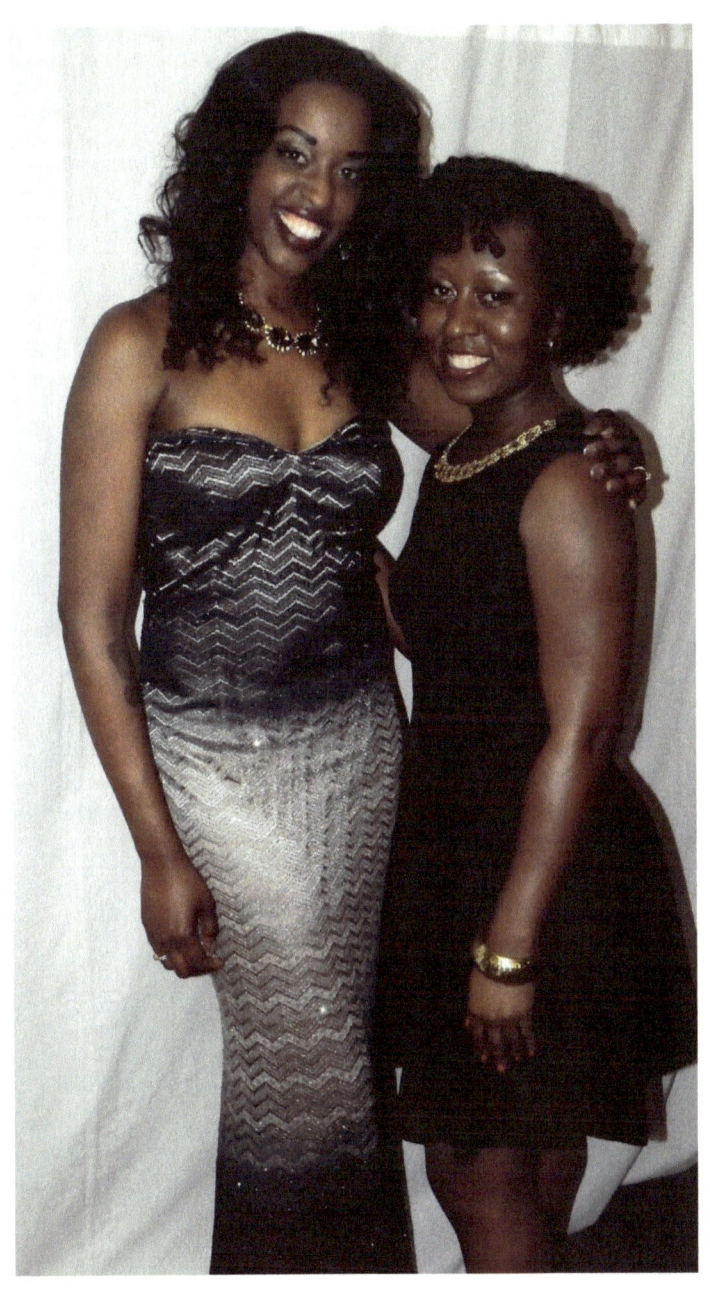

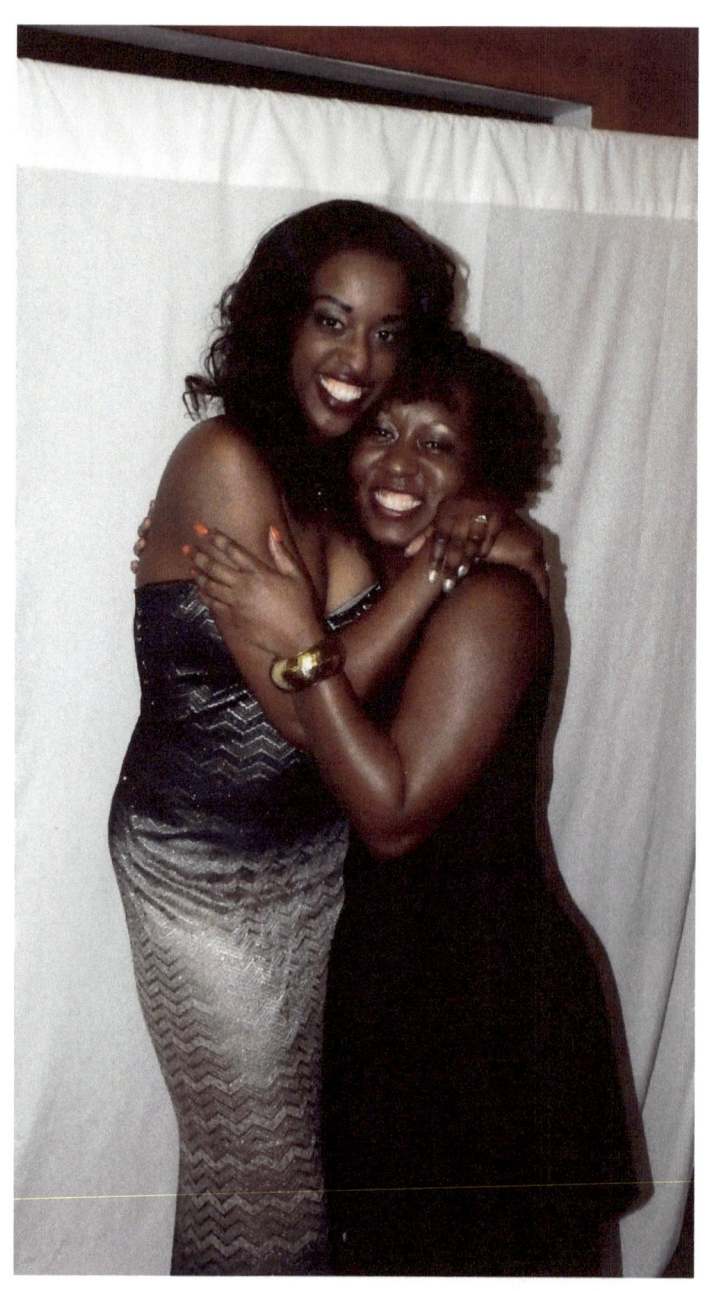

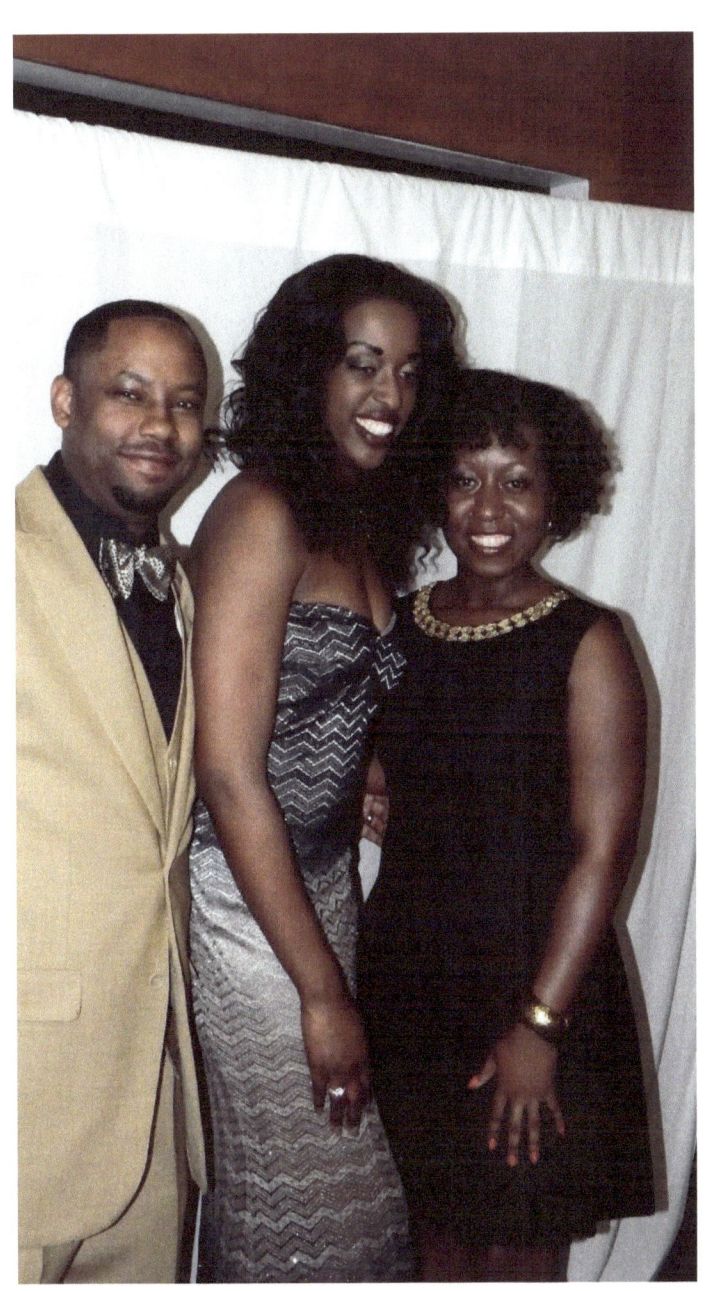

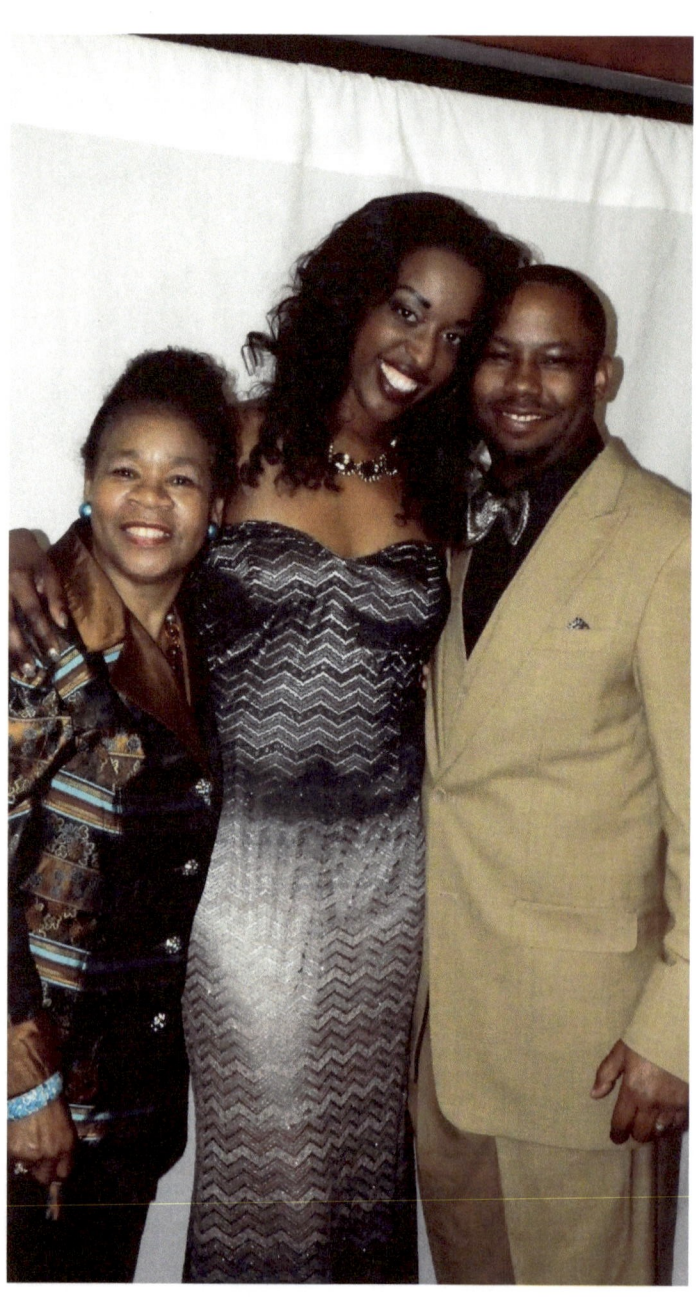

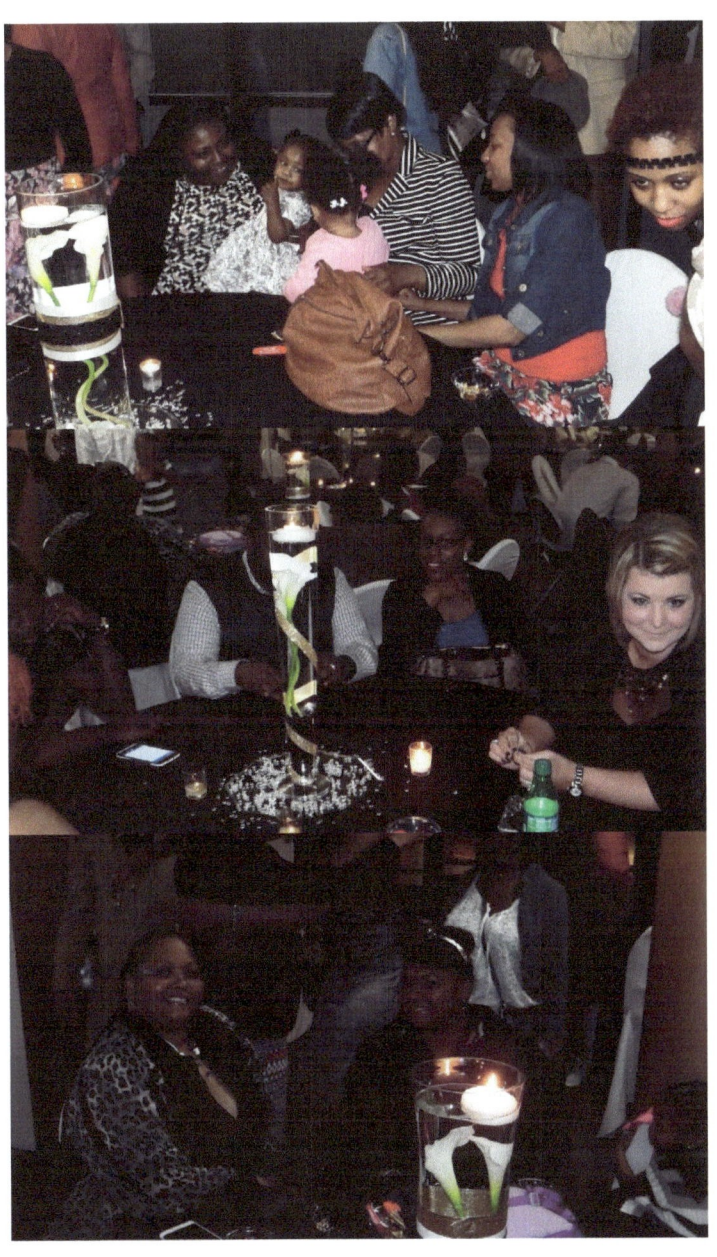

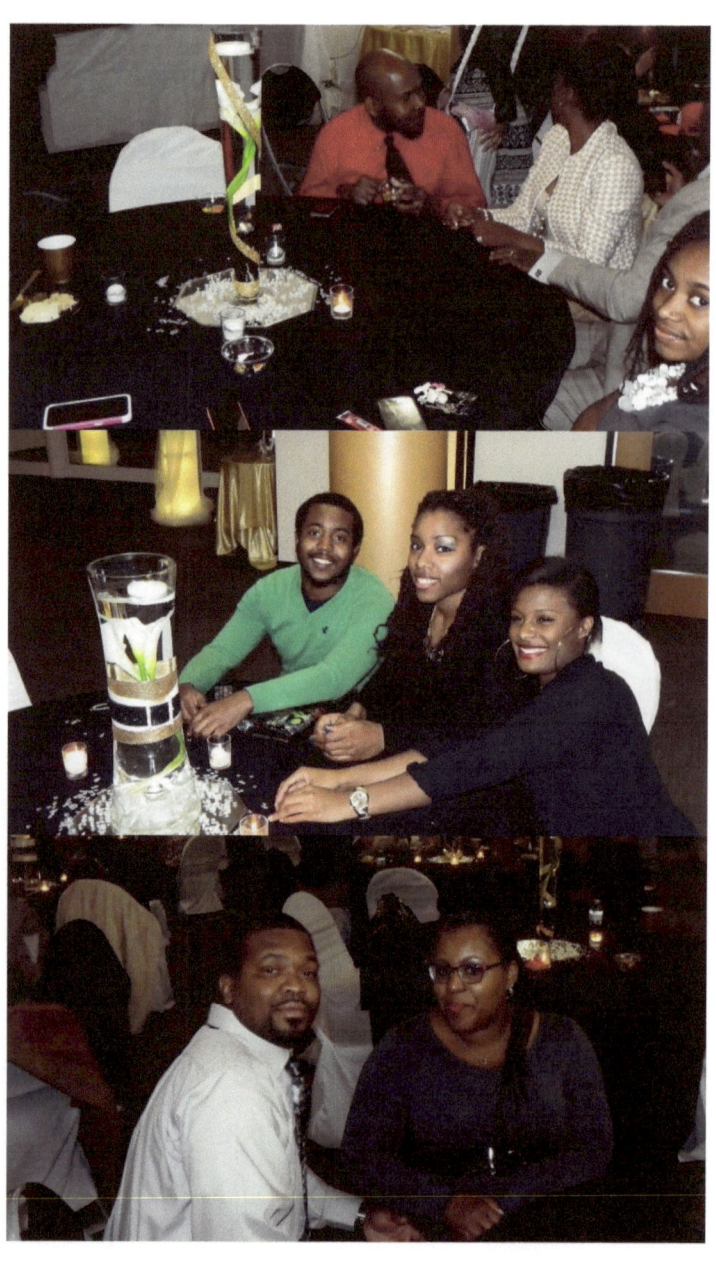

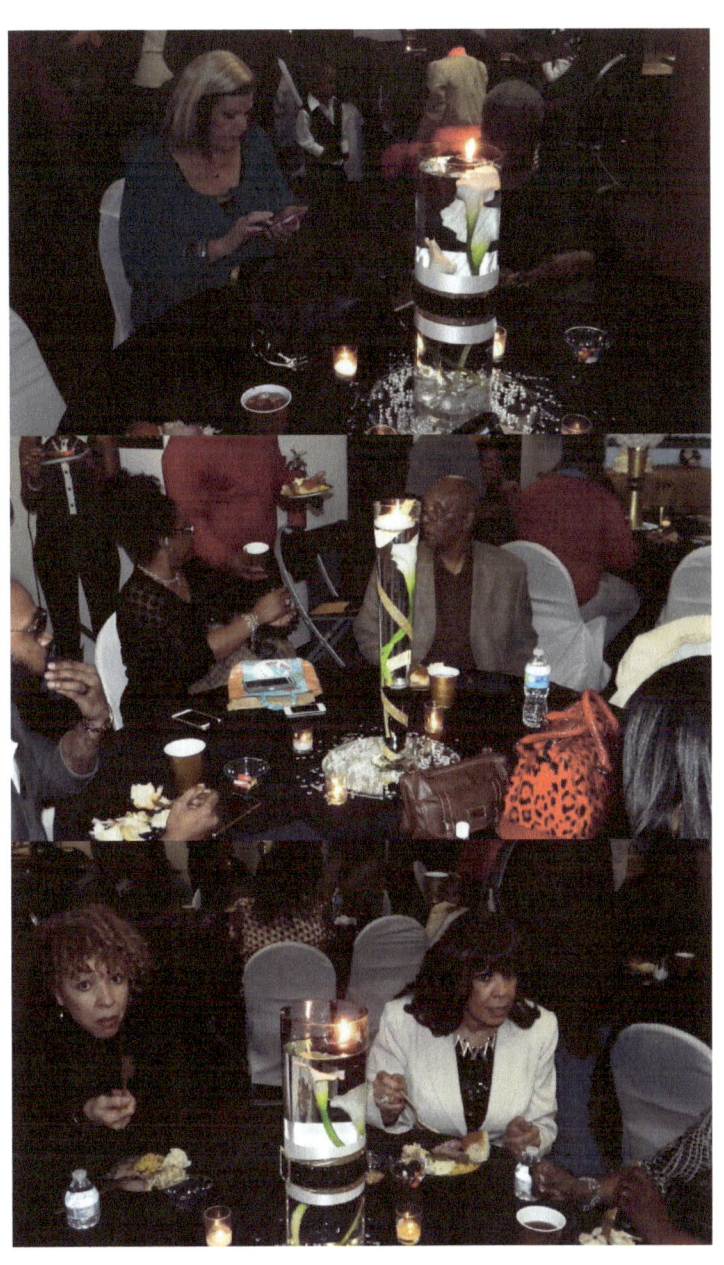

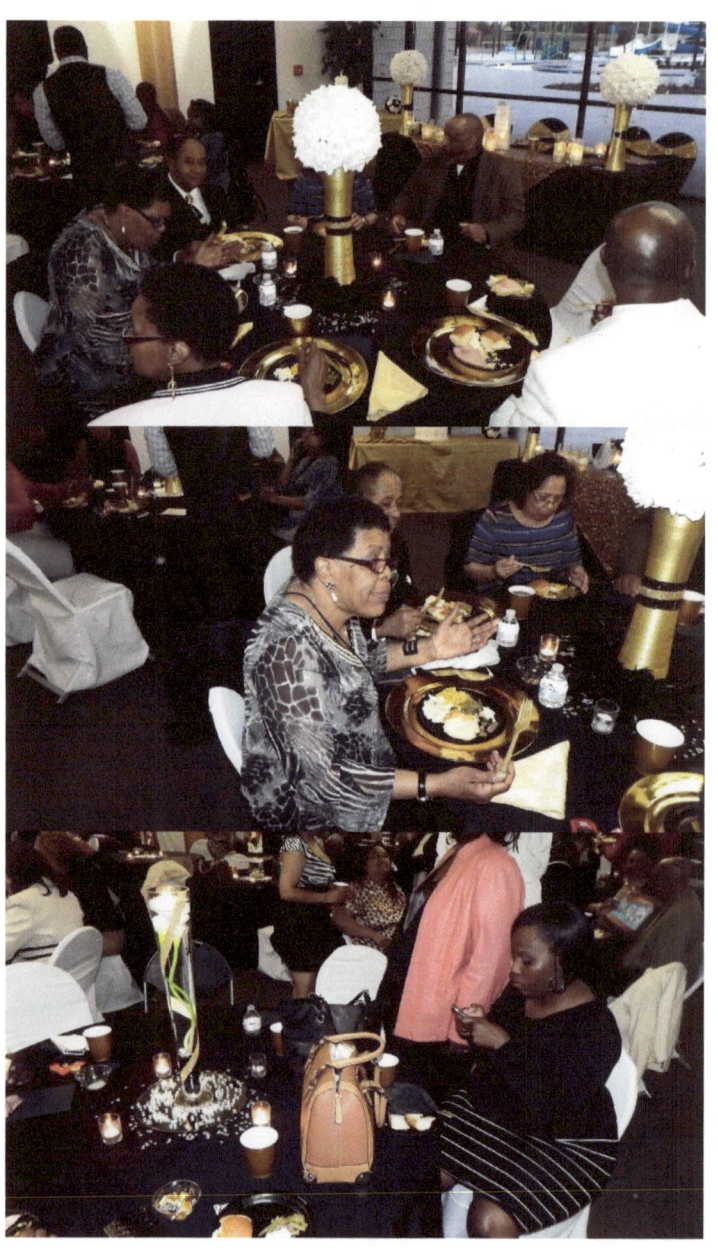

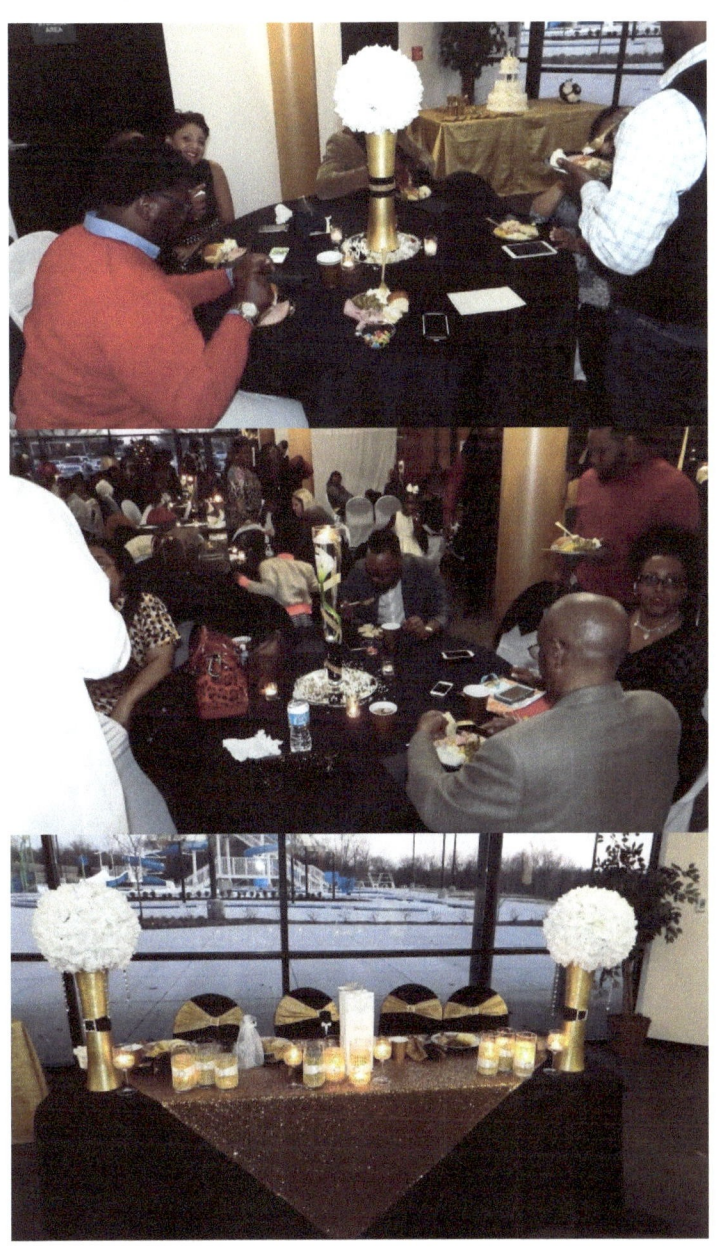

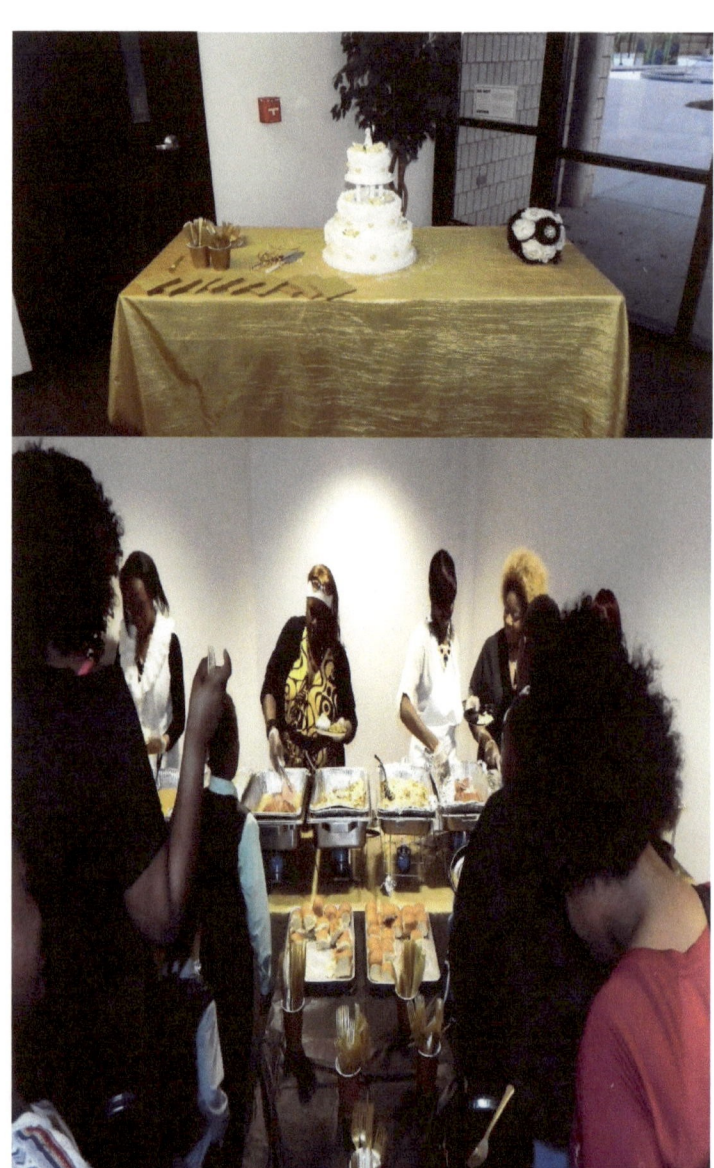

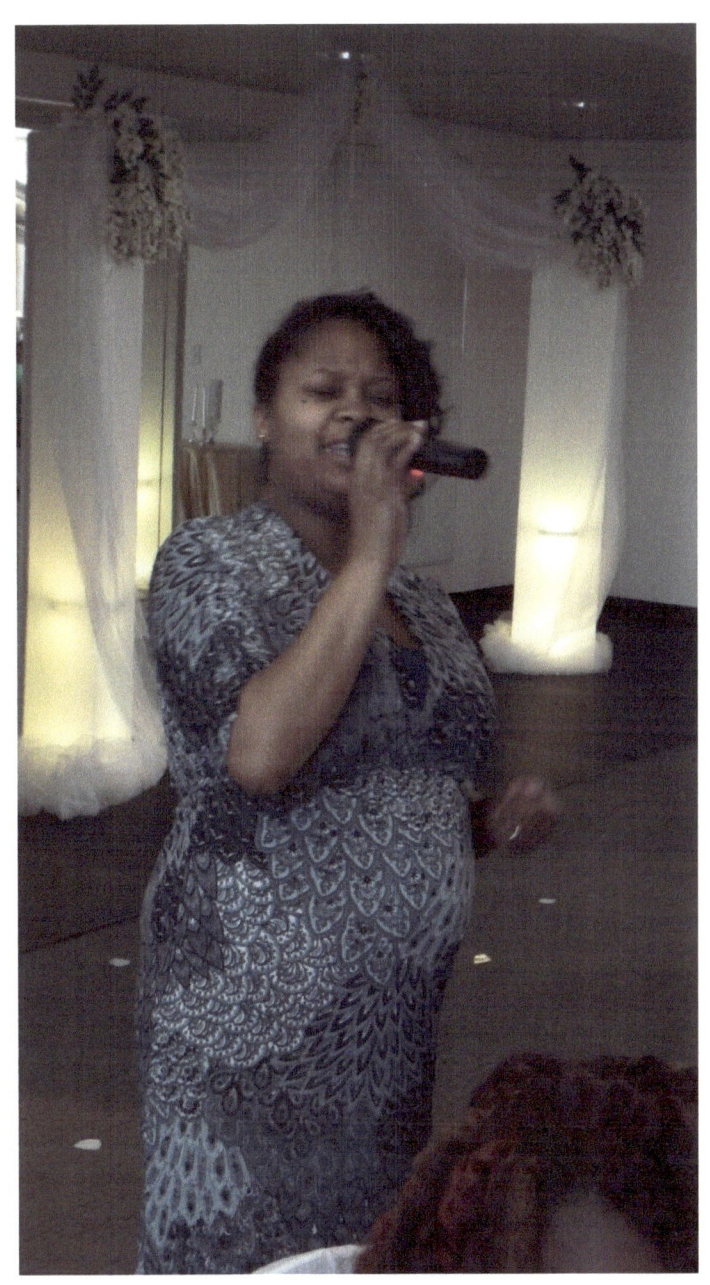

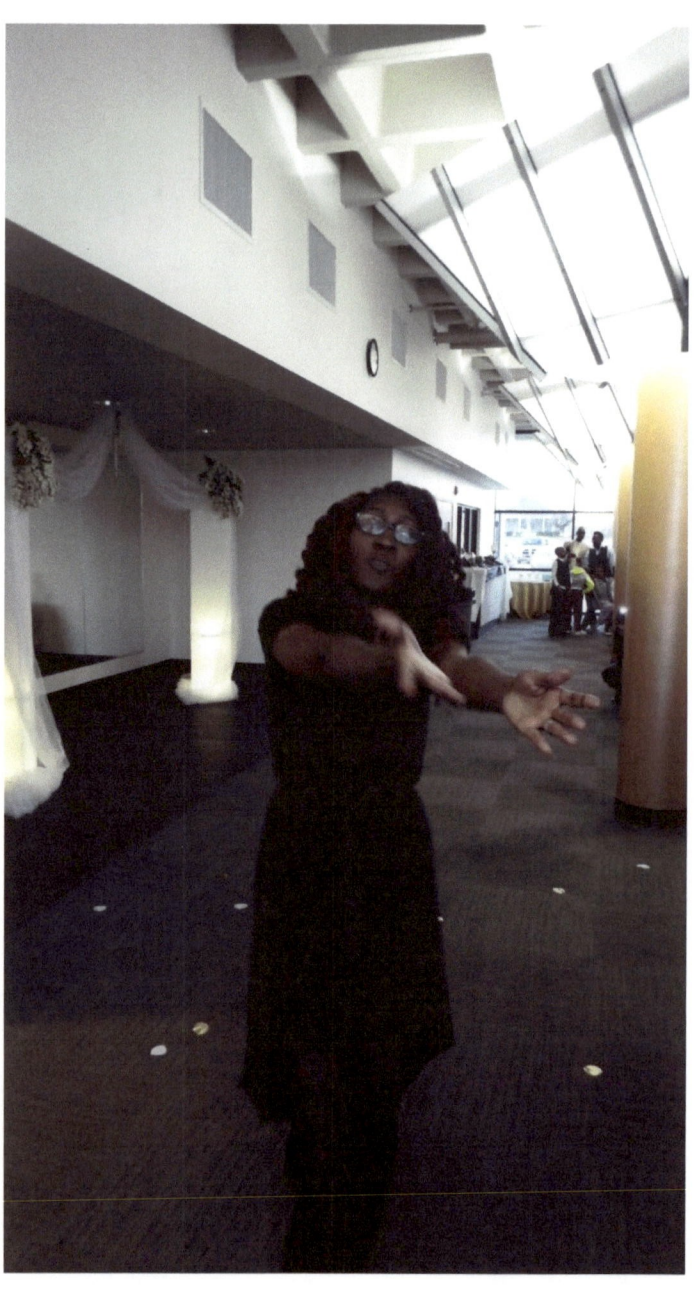

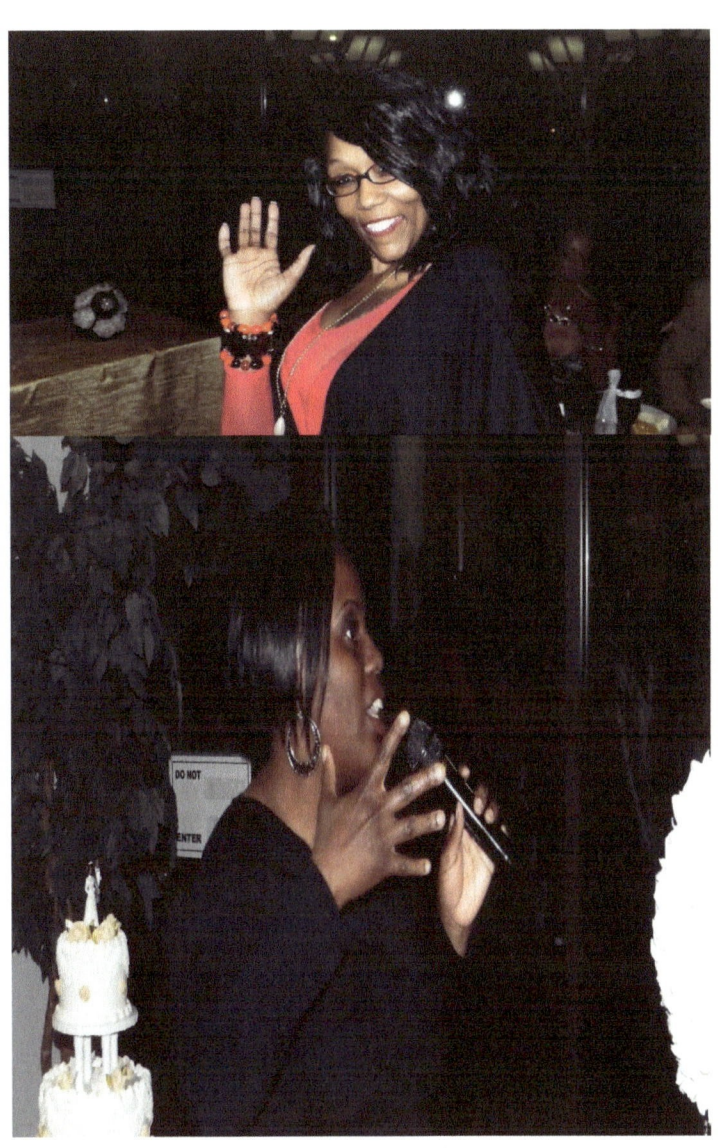

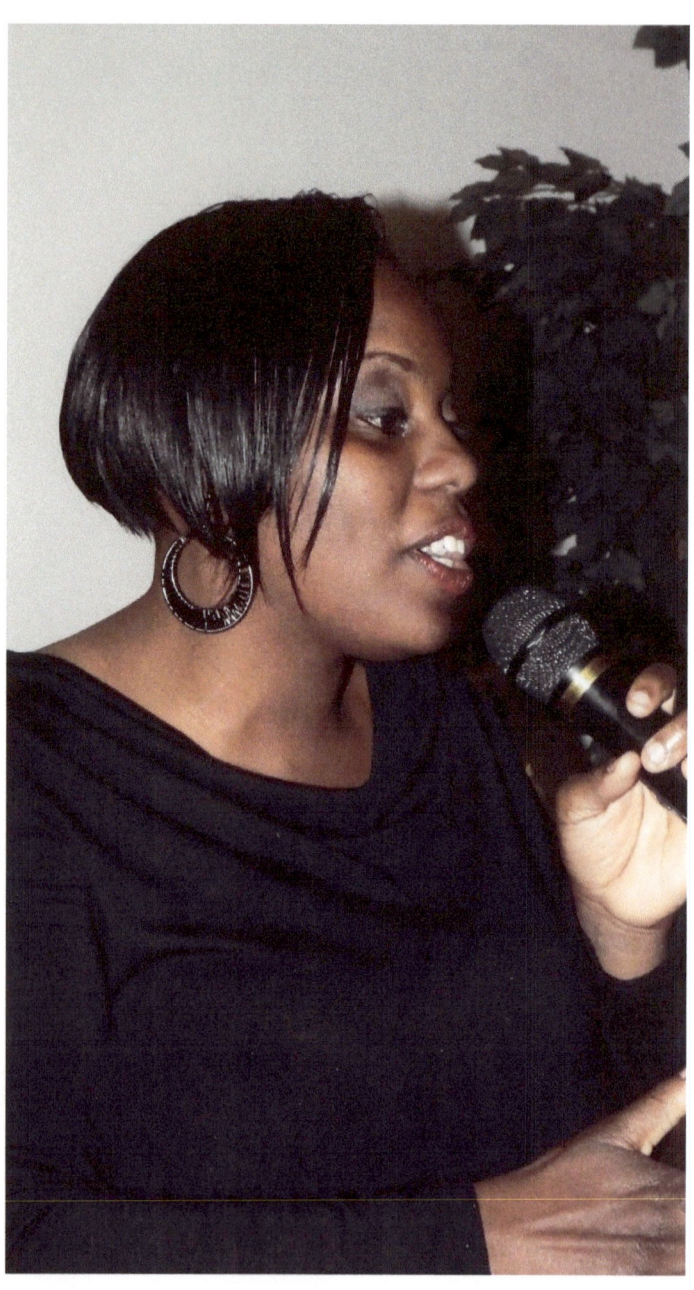

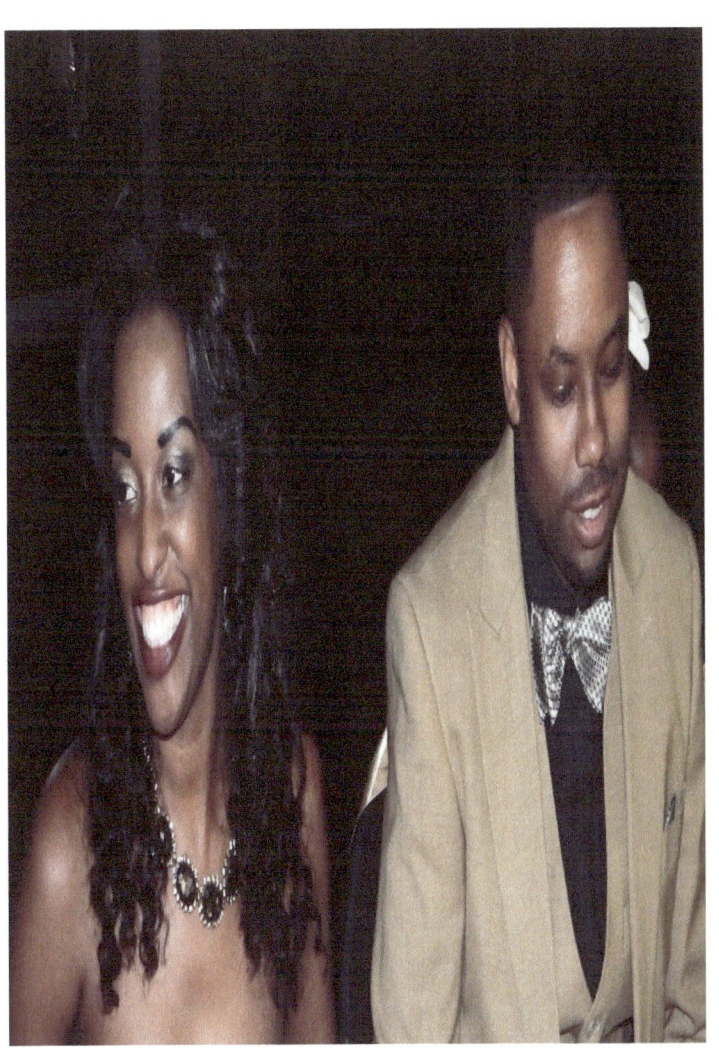

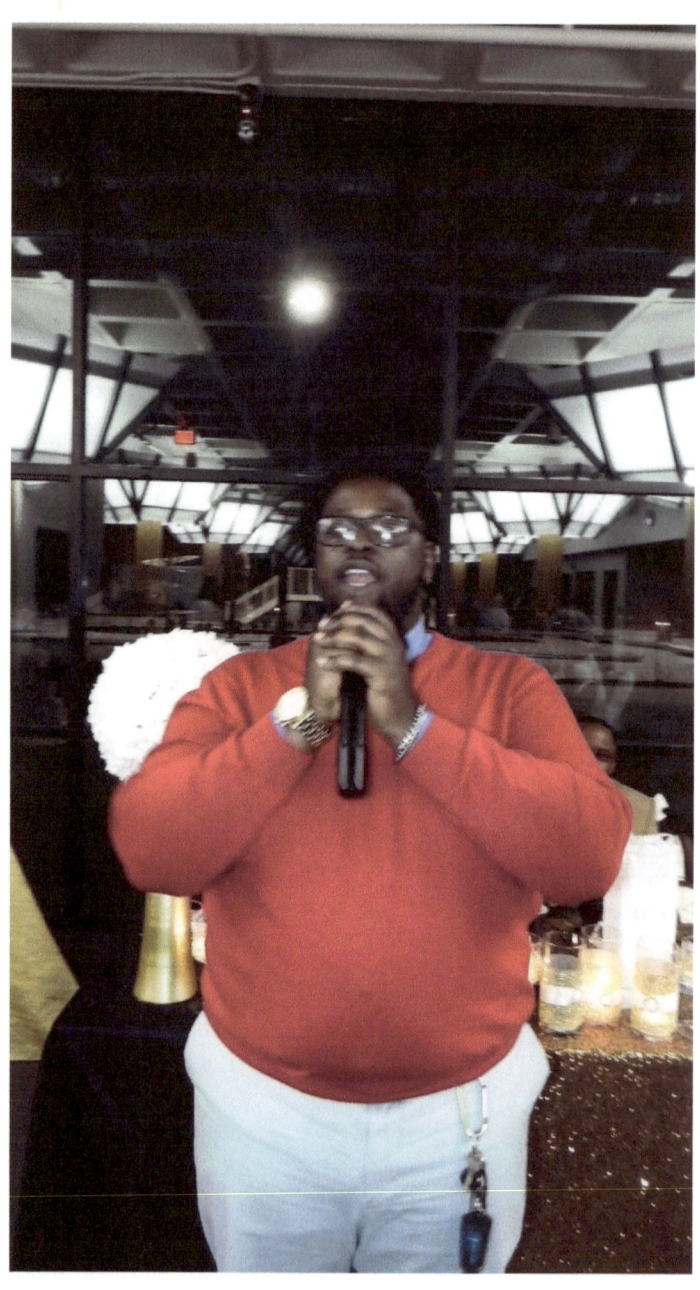

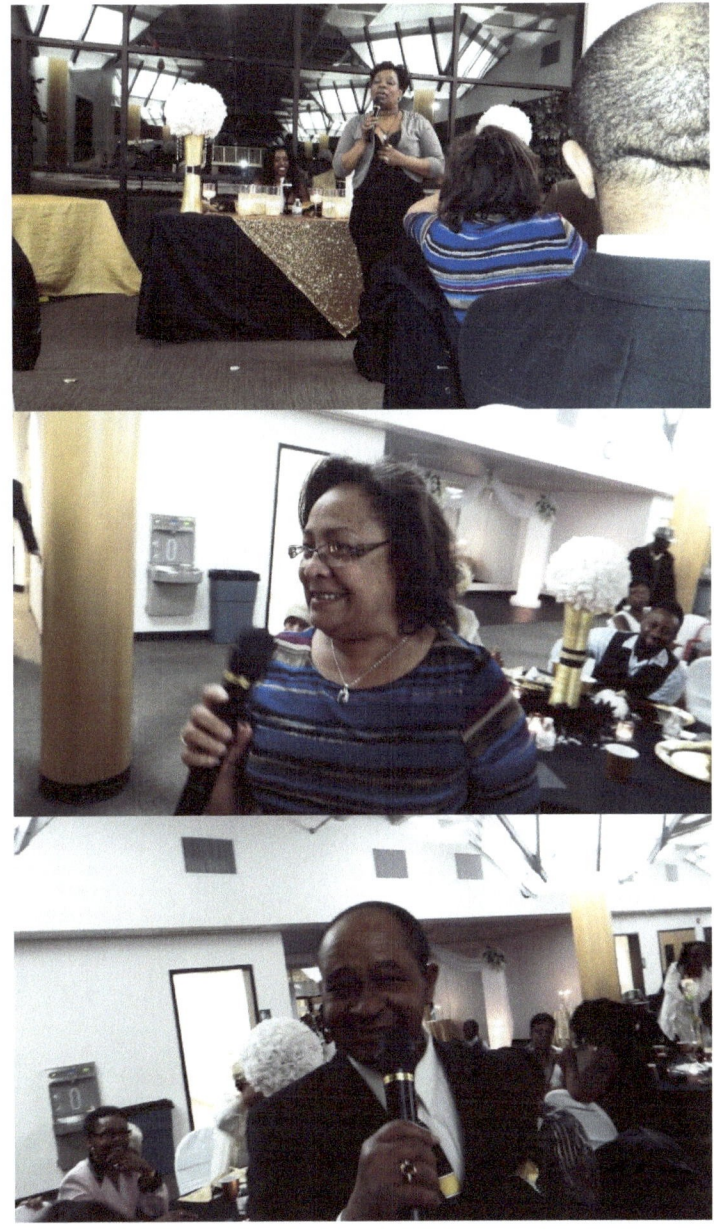

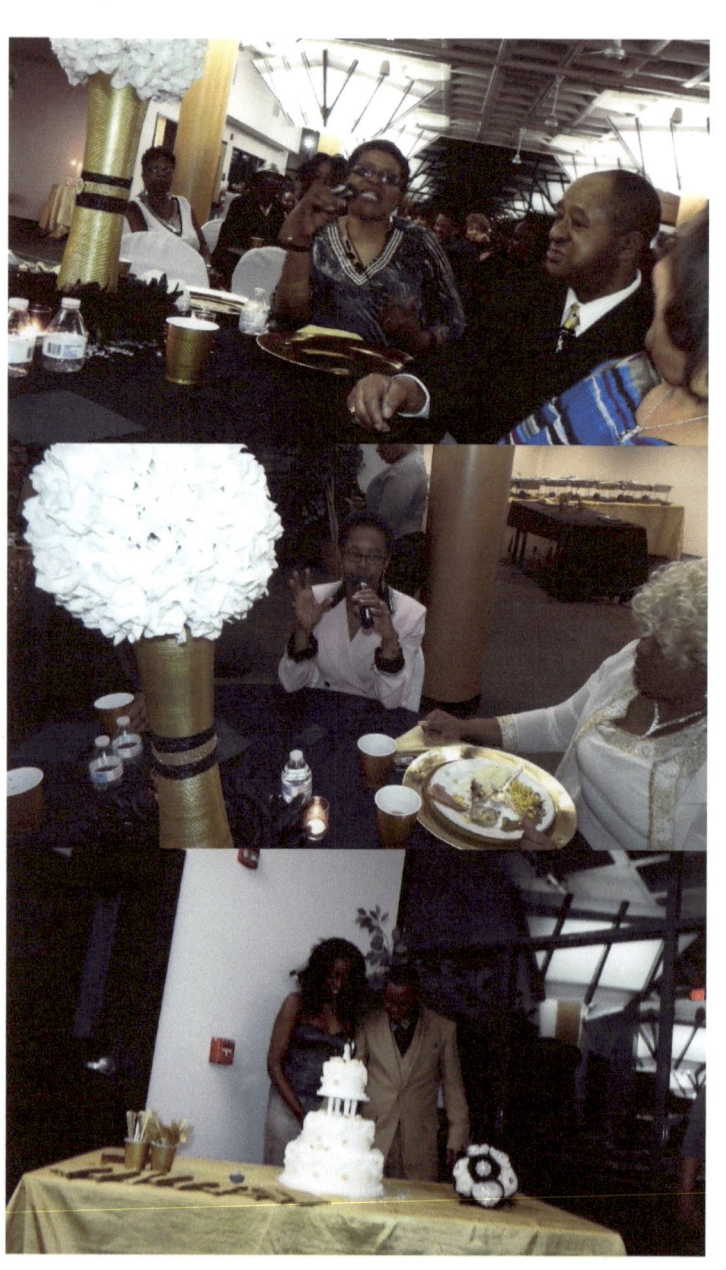

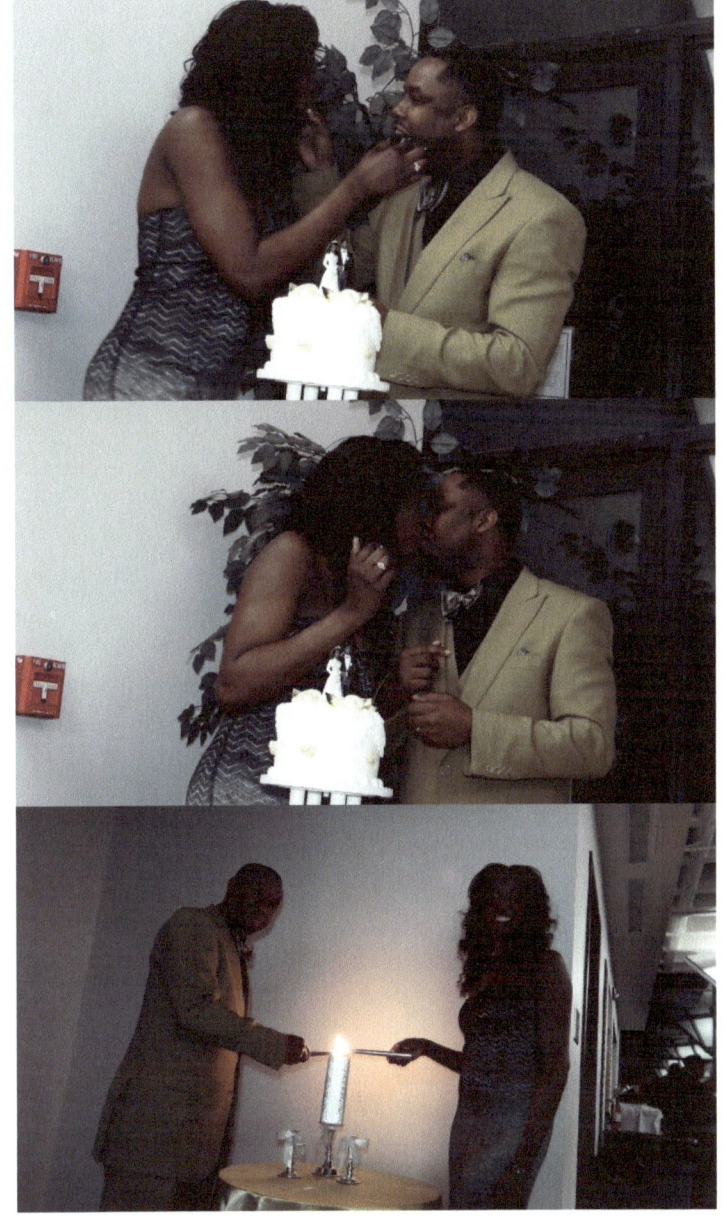

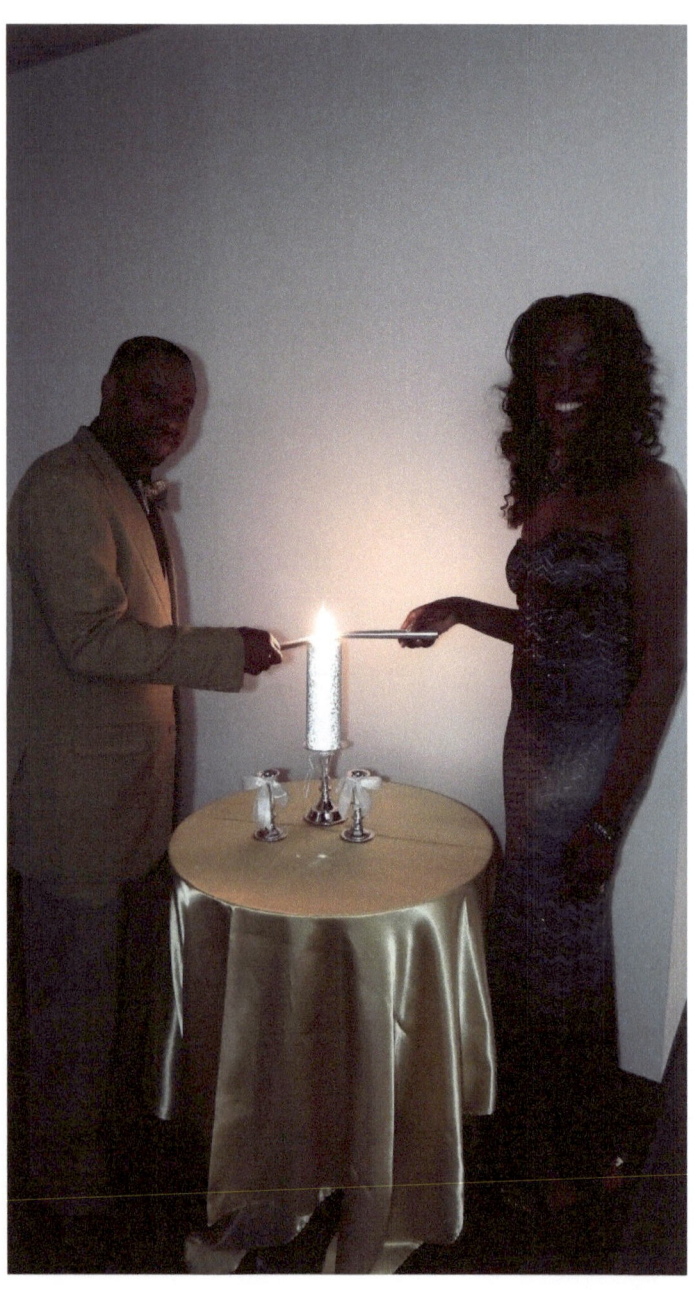

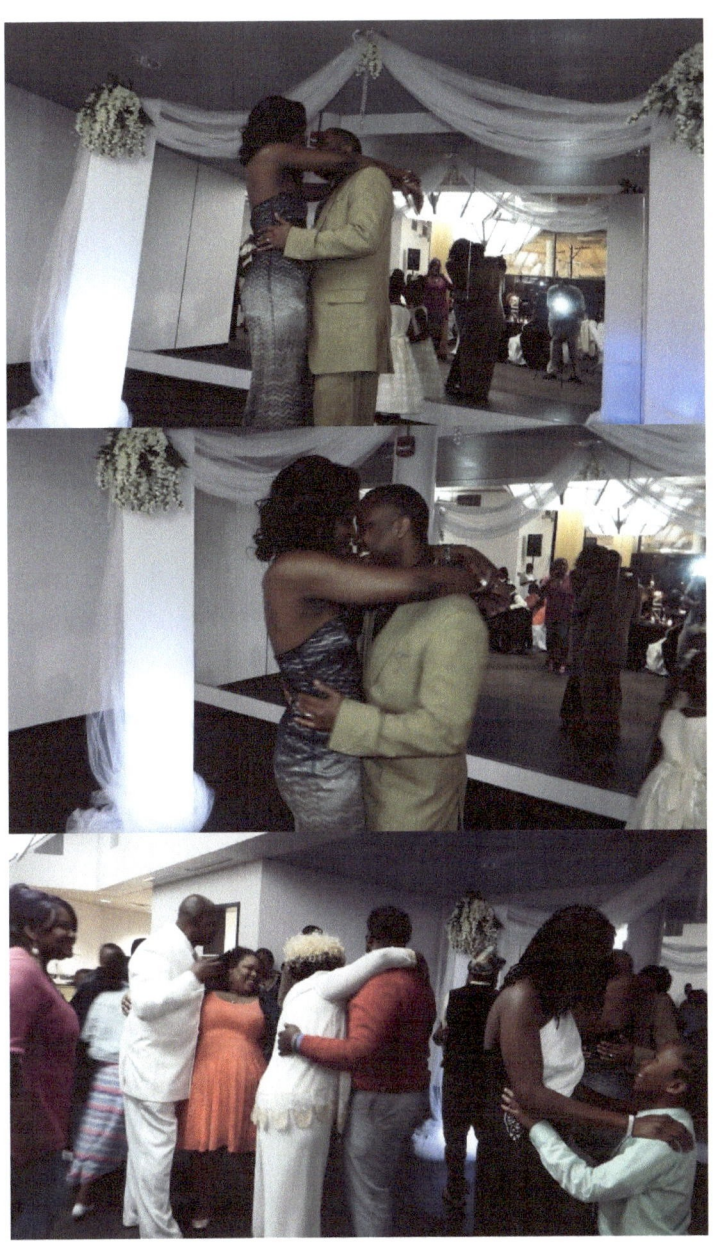

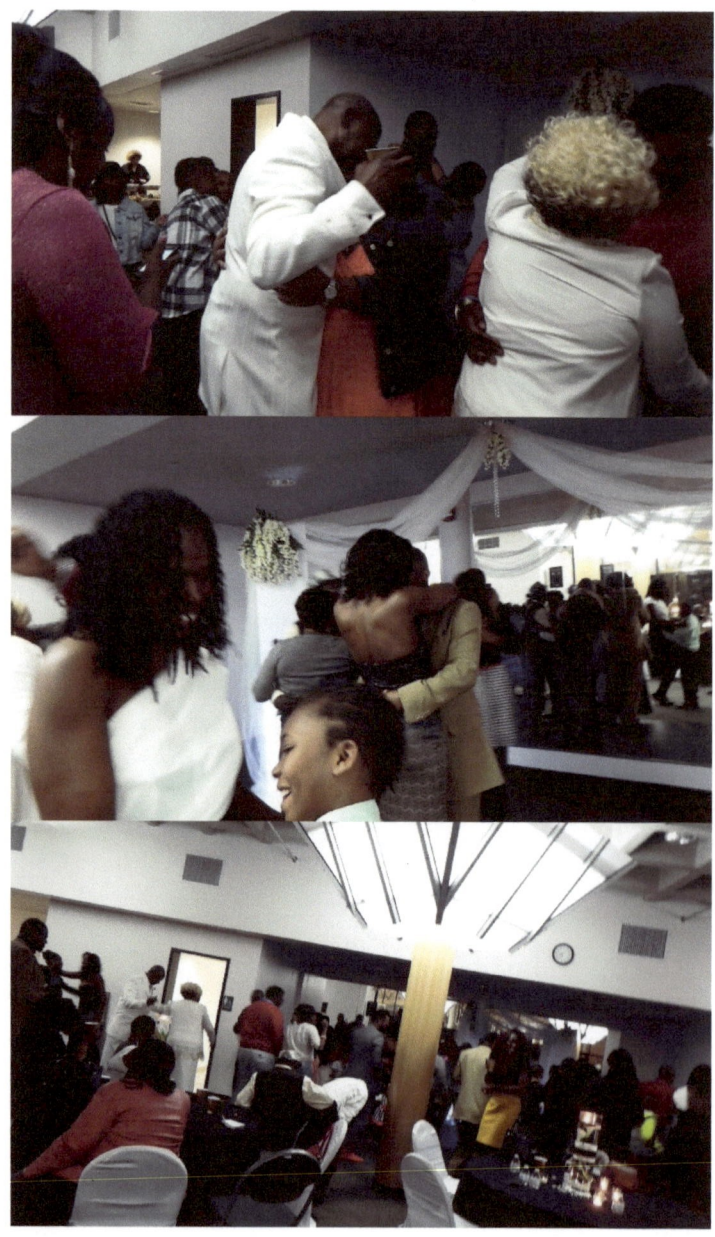

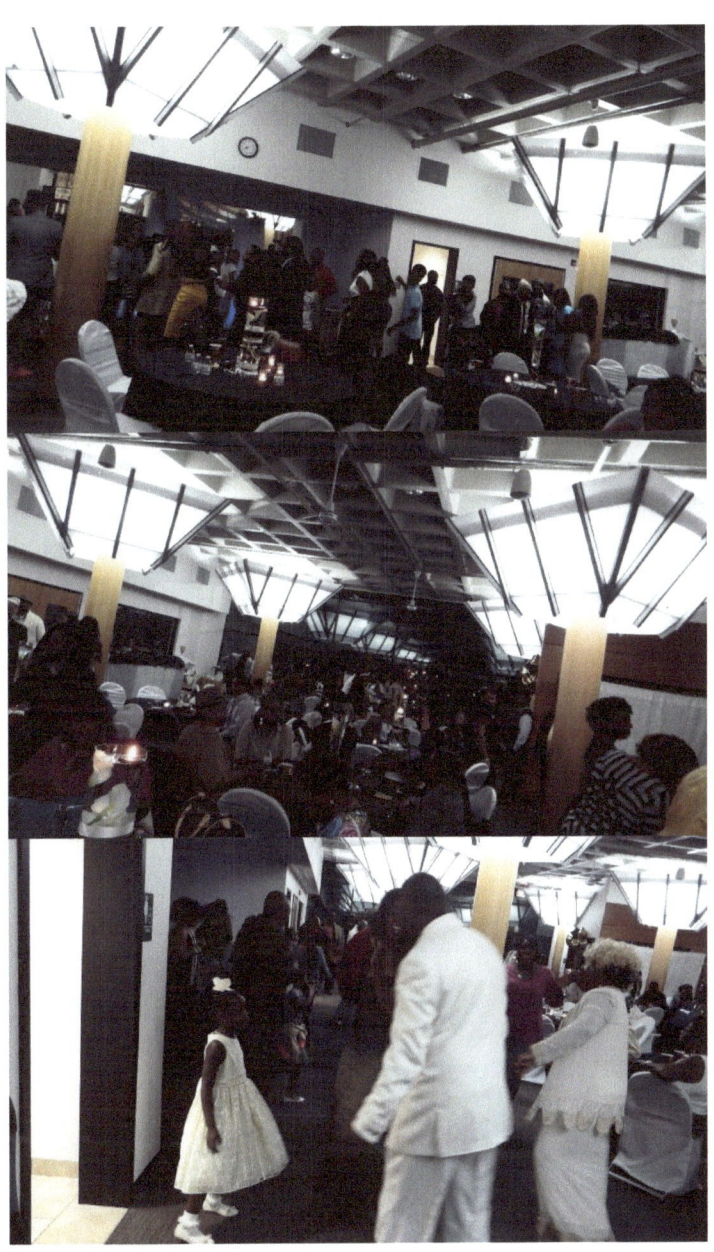

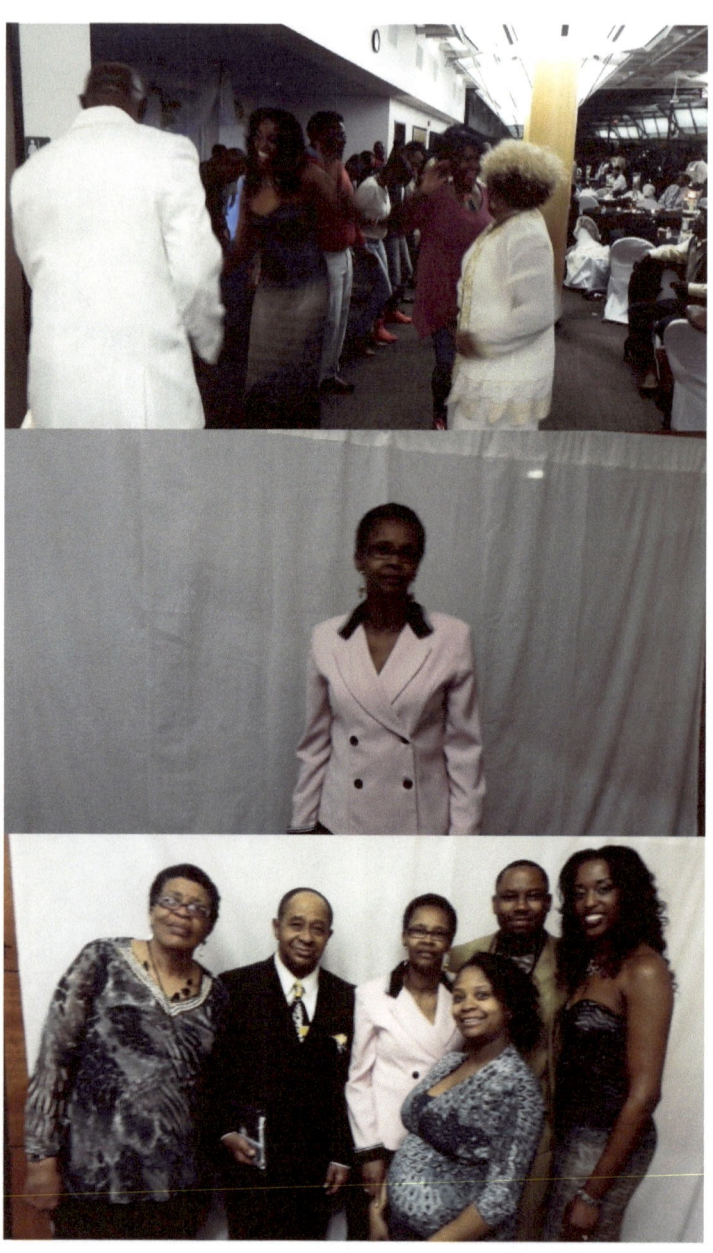

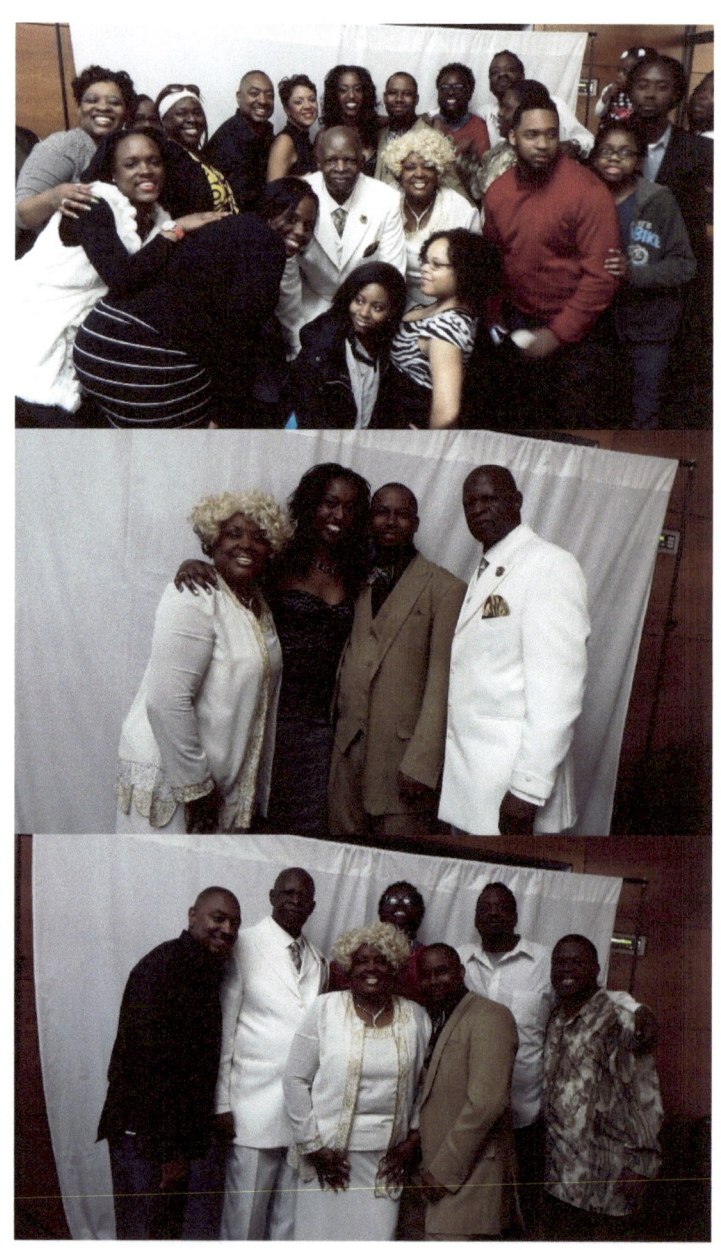

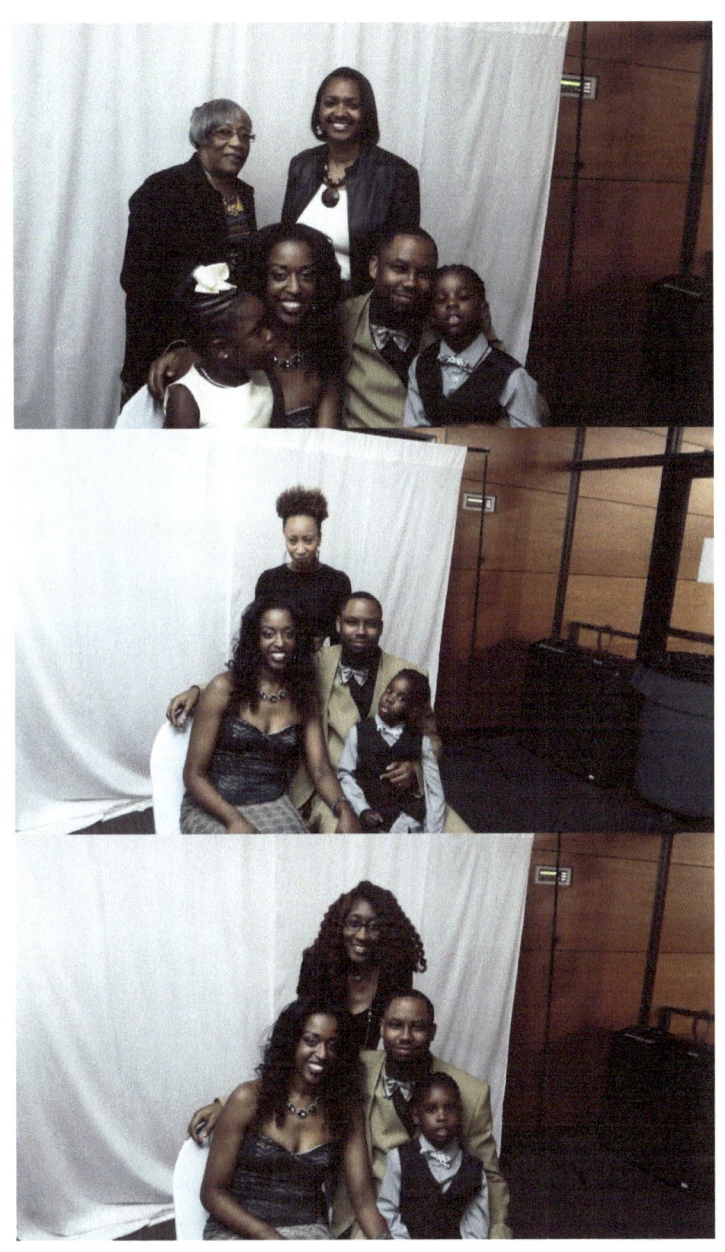

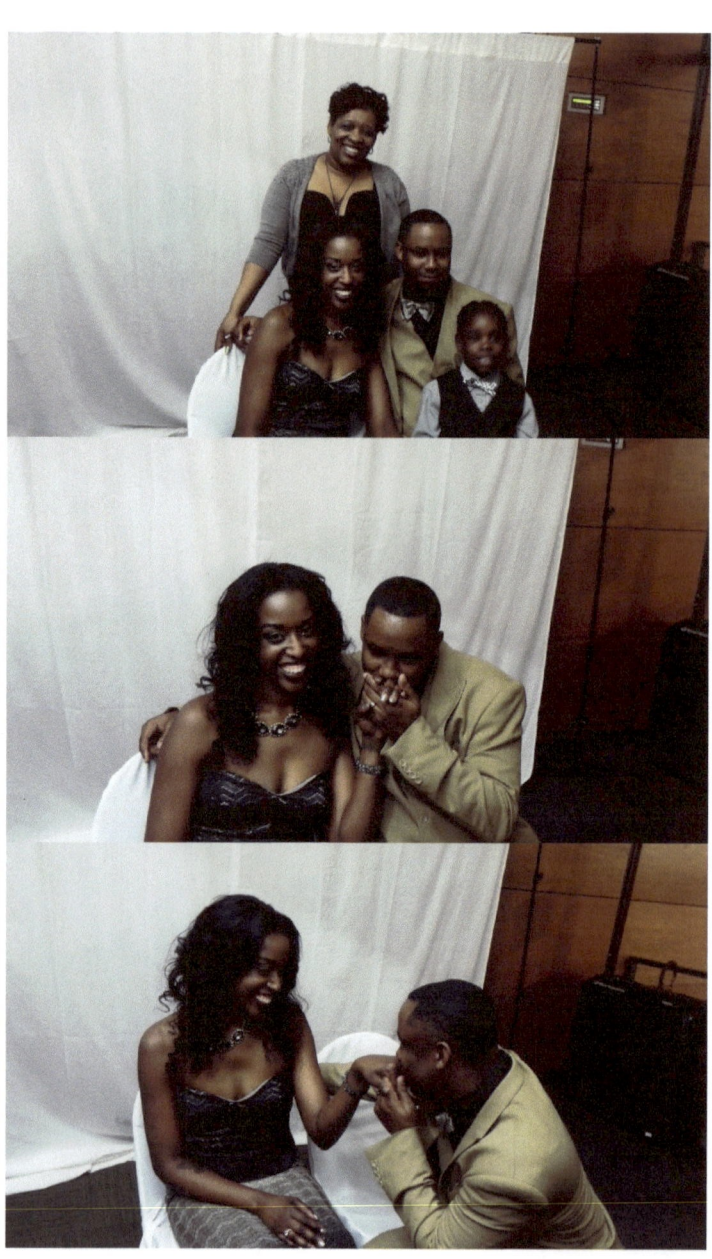

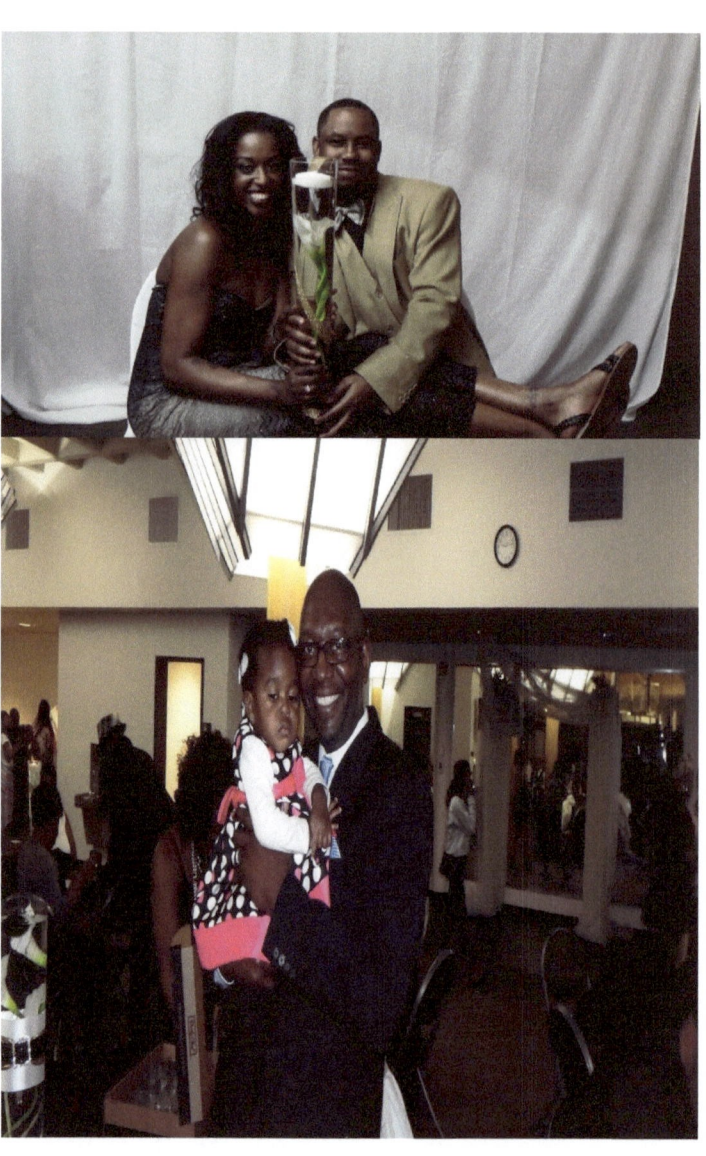

www.ingramcontent.com/pod-product-compliance
Lightning Source LLC
Chambersburg PA
CBHW040811200526

45159CB00022B/247